ENDORSEMENTS

I love tools, and this one is created by Sally Hanan, who is definitely a great coach. You can pay thousands of dollars for what is in this simple but profound workbook. The stories, the different points of view, her surveys, the stories of unique individuals, and the assessments all come together as you fill out the answers to her questions. As you assess yourself, you see the development in you that is really going to create a beautiful picture by the end of the book.

I love any books that help you perceive your value and understand yourself, but this goes to another level entirely--where Sally gives you a foundation to see yourself from God the Father's eyes. I highly recommend Sally's workbook, and all of her tools she has put together, to help you develop your inner perspective so you can have incredible outward impact on the world around you!

~ *Shawn Bolz,*
Author of Translating God *and* God Secrets,
Host of Exploring the Prophetic *podcast, www.bolzministries.com*

Coach Yourself
with the Father

Sally Hanan

Fire Drinkers Publishing

COACH YOURSELF
WITH THE FATHER

Copyright © 2018 by Sally Hanan

All rights reserved. No part of this publication may be reproduced, distributed, or transmitted in any form or by any means, including photocopying, recording, or other electronic or mechanical methods, without the prior written permission of the publisher, except in the case of brief quotations embodied in critical reviews and certain other noncommercial uses permitted by copyright law. For permission requests, write to the author, addressed "Attention: Permissions," at the e-mail address below.

alive@pickyourlife.com

Special discounts are available on quantity purchases by corporations, associations, and others. For orders by US trade bookstores and wholesalers, contact the author at the e-mail address above.

Unless otherwise marked, all Scripture quotations are from *The Holy Bible, English Standard Version*® (ESV®), copyright © 2001 by Crossway, a publishing ministry of Good News Publishers. Used by permission. All rights reserved.

All Scripture quotations marked AMP are taken from the Amplified® Bible (AMP), copyright © 2015 by The Lockman Foundation. Used by permission. www.Lockman.org

Editing services: Inksnatcher & Christi McGuire Creative Consulting
Cover & interior design/layout: Allison Metcalfe Design

First Edition, 2018
ISBN: 978-0-9913350-8-4
Publisher: Fire Drinkers Publishing

This book is dedicated to every person I have had the pleasure of meeting on this adventure called life. You have each left your mark of love, laughter, or learning on this heart. Thank you for being you.

Table of Contents

Foreword ix

I. WHO YOU ARE
1. Your Design 1
2. Your Mirror 13
3. Your Personality 27

II. WHAT YOU DO
4. Gifts & Talents 39
5. Knowledge & Experience 51
6. Spiritual Gifts 73

III. WHY YOU DO IT
7. Values 81
8. Passion 93
9. Dreams 107

IV. WHEN PURPOSE BEGINS
10. The Journey 129
11. Action 143
12. Legacy 155

About the Author 167

Foreword

In my first workbook, *Fix Yourself,* I take the reader through steps that make the heart whole. In my second workbook, *Empower Yourself,* I focus on how to hear God and be a conduit for the gifts of the Holy Spirit. This workbook, *Coach Yourself,* is for those who want to better their lives, to live life fully alive, and to max out life in every way so they can leave this world with nothing left unfinished.

I've split the book into four sections: who you are, what you do, why you do it, and when living out your life purpose begins. I start with an introduction to see yourself the way God does—the way he has done since you were a tiny idea in his ginormous mind. I then give you some tips on what you do and how to see it all from God's viewpoint. The section on why you do things teaches you how to understand the reasons for your being exactly the way you are. Lastly, in the when section, I talk about how you can live your life from here on out in a way that will fuel you and make God look good.

Each chapter opens with short testimonials from people on the chapter's topic. These are followed by some thoughts and insights of my own. The sections after that are interactive—between you and God. You'll find assessments, open-ended questions, and space to respond to particular Bible verses. Each chapter is then wrapped up with the life story (to date) of an interesting individual. Other than Shawn Bolz's story, I deliberately interviewed people without household names so you could identify with their God-rich lives.

We all matter, but it's often hard to know why when we live out our day-to-day existence according to a set schedule that never seems to change, apart from the occasional vacation or weekend away. I hope that by the end of this book, you'll see your life as a gift with limitless opportunities.

~ Sally

WHO YOU ARE

YOUR DESIGN

One thing I've learned about my design is that it is unique. I'm an identical twin, which means I've been called my sister's name many times in my life. Some people just called me Twin instead of my name, but we have our own fingerprints and personalities, and there are differences in how we look. A lot of people, on finding I have an identical twin, have said, "Oh, there are two of you." To which I've always responded, "No, there's one of me and one of her." So I think each of us has a deeply ingrained desire to be seen as her own design and person.

Another thing I know is that God saw what I wanted to do as a child and put it with the gifts he placed in me—long before I ever saw them. I learned that when he does the mixing together in the right time, it turns out to be a beautiful and fulfilling thing.

~ Sharon O.

My dad had a 16mm movie camera (wedding gift from my mom), so he made a movie of me, their firstborn. Amazing to see how he composed everything with that old technology, but as I recall seeing it, the titles went something like this: "Presenting Edythe Dorothea Thompson ... Produced by Alexander and Ruth Thompson ... (next frame) ... and GOD!"

~ Edy J.

God knows my design better than me, and I come closer to my true self in his presence in and through being with him, and knowing him better and better.

~ Mary L.

Before the beginning of time, when all the skills were being decided upon for everyone in the world, rumor has it when they got to my name, they said, "This one will be so good-looking, we have to balance that out—so no dancing, no skateboarding, no surfing, no golf, and no knitting." I weep sometimes, but not a lot....

~ Gerry H.

Who are you? Why does it even matter? Or more to the point, why do you matter?

One reason why you know you matter is because God took the time to come up with a very precise idea of you. The phrase "twinkle in your daddy's eye" could also be about the excitement he had when coming up with your design. You're not some random algorithm filling up space until you die. You are created by the master craftsman, and every single brain cell, every part of your soul, every bit of your spirit existed in God's mind long before you were ever born.

Some Christians would say it doesn't matter at all who you are, as long as you are fully surrendered to God and obey him explicitly. That's all fine and well for those who have a passion for rules and order, but many times that acceptance comes at the expense of love. Others might say it's all about the presence of God; nothing else matters, least of all you, you little peon, you. Which again makes me question the love part.

"I knew you" (Jeremiah 1:5). When you read that verse in Hebrew, the word "knew" implies an instinctive, all-knowing, fully immersed kind of knowledge. God knew and planned exactly what kind of gift you would be to the world; the thought and strategic markers that went into your blueprint were very deliberate.

God mentioned how he knew John the Baptist. "He will turn many of the children of Israel to the Lord their God, and he will go before him in the spirit and power of Elijah, to turn the hearts of the fathers to the children, and the disobedient to the wisdom of the just, to make ready for the Lord a people prepared" (Luke 1), and Paul (Galatians 1:15), and David (Psalm 139:15) before conception. He knew Jeremiah: "Before I formed you in the womb I knew you, and before you were born I consecrated you [set you apart]" (Jeremiah 1:5). I don't think it's a stretch to think he knew you in hefty detail before you were conceived as well.

God's knowledge of your blueprint was the deciding point for giving you life. When we cooks choose a recipe, we often do so because we like the photo of how it should turn out, but we cook in faith. God sees us as far more than a recipe before he breathes his life into us. He knows how we'll be, because everything he's put in us is perfectly measured for a person he wants and knows is needed in the world. He doesn't need a photo mixed with faith before he infuses us with life. He gives life to what he has deliberately planted in us.

> *So God created man in his own image, In the image of God he created him; ... And God blessed them. ... And God saw everything that he had made, and behold, it was very good.*
> *~ Genesis 1:31*

Artificial intelligence (AI) is a hot topic these days. If I had the means to build myself a robot, I'd make sure that once built, it would serve me well. If I was then told my creation would instead be my human child, one who would represent me on earth long after I'm gone, I'd make my plans less self-serving. I'd look at my child's world and implement abilities and brain patterns that would serve humanity well instead. Not only that, because it's obvious that one child couldn't do everything,

I'd give my future adult a skill set that could complement the skills in others perfectly. That way things would be done properly, and there would be a wholeness about the projects teams worked on together.

I'd give my female robot passion for certain projects so she would be filled with excitement when she was working on them. I'd make her personality one that worked well with the people she'd be around and gave her the best complementary skills for what needed to be accomplished. I'd give her delight in certain kinds of people and certain types of creativity. I'd figure out our communication channel and wire her to get the hang of it easily.

> *Life in God is not just about having faith in him. Did you know that he has faith in you, too? He is utterly convinced that you are going to be wonderful, exceptional, and brilliant as his child. And he is intentional about changing your perception of yourself to align with his. ~ Graham Cooke,* Kingdom Thinking Collection

God is all about relationship. He hasn't created hordes of robots; he's created sons and daughters, first and foremost so he could hang out with us. When he went into creative mode, he designed each of us with a unique personality, gifts, passions, and talents; and he knew what kind of knowledge and experience we'd pick up along the way. By the end of the planning stage, he was able to stand back and look at a plan well made—because we are designed in his image. Wonderful, exceptional, and brilliant were all in his vocabulary about us when he looked at us doing our unique thing and being our unique selves in our futures.

God knows what you're capable of because he's put you together. Now it's up to you to recognize everything that's gone into you and decide what to do with it.

> *What you are is God's gift to you, what you become is your gift to God. ~ Hans Urs von Balthasar,* Prayer

FINISH THESE SENTENCES

When I think about God knowing me before conception, I

Here's what I think of God's blueprint of me—the whole package:

When I think of God knowing me completely—body, soul, and spirit—I feel

I think God gave me life because

When I think about God creating me as one of his gifts to the world, I think

If God made me in his likeness, then

TRUTH

What is the truth about your perfect design? Mull over the following Scriptures and write down anything God shows you through them.

"Before I formed you in the womb I knew you." (Jeremiah 1:5)

"The Spirit of God has made me, and the breath of the Almighty gives me life." (Job 33:4)

"Worthy are you, our Lord and God, to receive glory and honor and power, for you created all things, and by your will they existed and were created." (Revelation 4:11)

"For everything created by God is good, and nothing is to be rejected if it is received with thanksgiving." (1 Timothy 4:4)

"Then God said, 'Let us make man in our image, after our likeness.' ... And God saw everything that he had made, and behold, it was very good." (Genesis 1:26,31)

THINK IT THROUGH, FIGURE IT OUT

If you got to design your child, what would you make sure was in the blueprint for him or her?

Personality

Gifts and talents

Life experience

Knowledge

When you think of God designing you as his child, how does his list compare with yours?

YOUR DESIGN

Imagine yourself as a living house. God comes in to rebuild that house. At first, perhaps, you can understand what He is doing. He is getting the drains right and stopping the leaks in the roof and so on; you knew that those jobs needed doing and so you are not surprised. But presently He starts knocking the house about in a way that hurts abominably and does not seem to make any sense. What on earth is He up to? The explanation is that He is building quite a different house from the one you thought of—throwing out a new wing here, putting on an extra floor there, running up towers, making courtyards. You thought you were being made into a decent little cottage: but He is building a palace. He intends to come and live in it Himself. ~ C.S. Lewis, Mere Christianity

SARAH'S JOURNEY (EARLY TWENTIES)

I was raised in a Christian household with two loving parents who homeschooled my brother and me. Between church activities and school, I had a great childhood. Unfortunately, under the shelter of home, family, and the church, I was molested at the age of five. I have blocked the details, but I do remember my parents crying over me and apologizing for not paying more attention to me. I learned years later that forgiveness is the most liberating thing that your heart will do, if you let it. I surrendered to compassion and forgave those who had wounded me.

When I was little my parents would explain to me the importance of saving yourself for the one God has chosen for you, and I believed that if I followed the rules, my happily ever after would come. But I felt that my fairytale was already stolen from me. I had been pushed into the mud by force, and even though I was pulled out, I could still find dirt under my nails. My parents talked about this feeling of "just knowing" when you have found the one, so I challenged myself to wait until I "just knew." On my thirteenth birthday, I bitterly told God that I wanted my first love to be my only love. Year after year went by as I watched everyone around me get hurt by failed relationships. I began to feel that maybe there was no such thing as "the one" and that maybe love was something you chose to feel for someone you enjoyed hanging out with. "Love" did not seem like it was worth the attempt, so I decided to focus on my career. Forever.

Right after my eighteenth birthday, I moved to start a job in another state. The plan was to build a career and live happily ever after. Little did I know that fifteen months after my move, my best friend would fall in love with me. And shockingly, I fell for him. I did not choose to feel love for him; I just felt it. I actually tried choosing not to feel it, because even though he was the most beautiful soul I had ever known, he was also a recovered heroin addict with a very different background than mine. But there was no denying that we just fit, so I let myself fall. It was the moment when he asked, "Theoretically, how long do you want to date before marriage?" that I just knew.

Life can completely change in a single moment. One day I received a call from his mom, saying that my boyfriend had decided to say a final goodbye to his old life by taking one last hit. He did not know that this last hit would take his last breath. Nobody deserves to feel the kind of pain that I felt that day, yet I discovered that so many do. I am learning to see the joy in the world again, and I have learned that seeing the value in another is never something to doubt. He was worth the wait, because now I know that love is real. All I want now is to bring joy to those who have felt a suffering too terrible to name.

Notes

Notes

YOUR MIRROR 2

When I was younger, I compared myself to pretty, skinny girls (when I was depressed), and when I was less depressed, to myself. When I was raising children, the standard was other mothers, because despite the prevailing view of my culture at the time (conservative Christians), I was a full-time working mother and my children were turning out pretty damn good, despite it.

~ Jan A.

When I feel anxious (and very anxious) is when I feel like I'm squandering time. I guess I feel that way when I'm not on top of things and I see another woman who is. When I'm right, what others are doing is encouraging, and when I'm not right, what others are doing is anxiety filling.

~ Lisa M.

Many years ago I was legalistic, so I compared my standards to others'. I didn't wear pants, had long hair, read the King James, listened to hymns only, etc. I was pretty good at following the rules, so I was a little better than many people. I was also pretty good at judging. I'm rolling my eyes at how I used to think. Over time, the Lord freed me of that mind-set. I'm having a hard time thinking of how I compare myself now. I might compare situations, since I've been in difficult circumstances for some years now, but I care less about what others think of me than I used to, and I don't have the energy to try to be anyone else but me anyway.

~ Laurie G.

As a teen, it was the popular girls I wanted to be like. I was always close to being in the popular girls' group, but somehow just outside that imaginary line. As an older woman, I compare myself to those women of my age who are always on the ball with their chores at home, and at the same time busy helping others, and at the same time having lots of women they can call to have coffee with or go to a movie with, and at the same time nurturing and involving themselves in their talents and hobbies while they are growing spiritually by leaps and bounds. I don't want too much ... just to be like them.

~ Lee M.

Most of us have lists, mirrors, and standards we feel we must measure up to, and if we don't, we've failed. But who gave us those mirrors? Who got to decide what went into the box marked "acceptable" and the one marked "failure?" We did! We decided that dressing or looking or acting a certain way was the acceptable way to be. We let our upbringing, cultural standards, friends, work environment, and social media determine what we needed to do to be *normal*. As if normal is something to aspire to.

Don't compare yourself with anyone in this world ... if you do so, you are insulting yourself. ~ Bill Gates

Michael Finkel, in his book *Stranger in the Woods* about Christopher Knight, a man who lived alone in the woods for twenty-seven years, quoted Knight as saying, "When I applied my increased perception to myself, I lost my identity. There was no audience, no one to perform for. There was no need to define myself. I became irrelevant." In Knight's case, removing himself from community is what made him irrelevant to everyone but strengthened his relevancy to himself.

When we know ourselves the way God does and embrace it rather than run the constant race to be like "that person," we begin to settle into our skins better. We understand how to relate to our communities—our spheres of family, friends, and coworkers. We give of ourselves comfortably, because once we've accepted ourselves, we think of ourselves less. We worry less about what others are thinking about us and care more about how valued they feel in our space. As one friend put it, "Needing approval from man means I don't know how awesome I already am."

Paul challenged the Corinthians to say he was irrelevant when he knew he wasn't: "I am not in the least inferior to these super-apostles" (2 Corinthians 11:5), and he knew he was relevant because of the number of changed lives around him. Liars were trying to pull believers away from the truth by twisting the message to fit their own need for recognition and funding, so Paul fell to espousing everything that made him the real deal.

He knew he was unskilled in speaking but full of knowledge.

He knew he loved the believers.

He knew what he'd gone without so unbelievers could have the truth.

He knew he had a bad temper (what I believe was his thorn in the flesh).

He was not embarrassed by any of his weaknesses, and he delighted in the knowledge and love God had given him. His lack of focus on himself made it easy for him to give his all. He lived in "the fullness of him who fills all in all" (Ephesians 1:23), but he played the comparison game for the Corinthians because that was the measure they were using.

What's so wrong with being unique? As we've experienced in the classroom, people mock those who are different—the nerdy, the loud, the questioning, the shy, those who dress differently. And those who get to decide the norm are the ones everyone wants to be like. If you can get just close enough to that standard, maybe people will see you, like you, and value you too. There's a problem with that though. Altering your perfectly designed self to fit someone else's means diminishing yourself. And why would you do that to something God has declared to be wonderful? Mordecai had the same perspective about everyone's life, and that was before Jesus even showed up on the scene to give his perspective. Mordecai told Esther, "Who knows whether you have not come to the kingdom for such a time as this?" (Esther 4:14).

> *Your dreams come crushing down when you tow the wrong path by looking at what others are doing. The Milky Way Galaxy would have been crushed down by now if each planet had left its own orbit to revolve elsewhere!*
> *~ Israelmore Ayivor,* Daily Drive 365

"I set you apart" (Jeremiah 1:5). We're all set apart to be fully us. Paul knew who he was and what he was on earth for. His heart was in good shape, he was empowered by the Holy Spirit, and he was able to just *be*. He was on earth for a set time, for a set number of years, to do what he would naturally do with his nature, his personality type, and his mix of natural and learned gifts and talents—all flowing through his state of oneness with his Father. He knew he had been designed before conception to live his life in tune with the things God had set him apart for *as Paul*.

YOU'RE set apart as you.

YOU'RE not better than or less than.

YOUR true identity and value is found in the One who designed and made you.

YOU'RE enough.

FINISH THESE SENTENCES

The number of things I need to accomplish before I feel acceptable is

The standards I mostly try to hold myself up to are found in

When I temporarily manage to live up to a standard I've set for myself, I feel

When I look at myself and the way I live my life from the outside, the way I think others do, I think

When I think about letting myself stand out and putting my unique self on display with no apologies, I think/feel

If I were to stop letting the way others live their lives dictate my own, my life would be

TRUTH

What is the truth about your mirror? Mull over the following Scriptures and write down anything God shows you through them.

"Not that we dare to classify or compare ourselves with some of those who are commending themselves. But when they measure themselves by one another and compare themselves with one another, they are without understanding." (2 Corinthians 10:12)

"For am I now seeking the approval of man, or of God? Or am I trying to please man? If I were still trying to please man, I would not be a servant of Christ." (Galatians 1:10)

"The Lord sees not as man sees: man looks on the outward appearance, but the Lord looks on the heart." (1 Samuel 16:7)

"Do not be conformed to this world, but be transformed by the renewal of your mind, that by testing you may discern ... what is good and acceptable and perfect." (Romans 12:2)

THINK IT THROUGH, FIGURE IT OUT

What does the perfect man or woman look like to you in regards to

Looks

Christian life—with God and in ministry

Work

Self-development

Physical health

Relationships

Character

Community

Would you ever impose these standards on anyone, including yourself?

If you think back to the child you got to create in a previous exercise, how many of these standards would you impose on him or her before it would be safe for that child to look in the mirror?

SHAWN'S BOLZ'S JOURNEY (LATE THIRTIES)

I grew up in a home that celebrated me and instilled a belief that I could do or be anything. My parents had never been nurtured to accomplish their life goals, though, so I had a big learning curve and some hurdles in the way of going after my life ambition. They expressed love but didn't know how to help me pursue the education or opportunities I felt so passionate about. Their support was worth so much though.

By nature, I was deeply insecure growing up but hid it behind my genuine, extrovert personality. I had to spend years becoming comfortable with myself and therefore presenting myself correctly to the world around me. A lot of this happened after my first season of successful public speaking and ministry. I had enough talent and gifts to realize I was good, but not enough to feel like I was excelling, so I ran after personal growth. I became a self-improvement junkie and killed insecurity by being vulnerable with it to the people, and sometimes public crowds, I shared life with.

I knew I was called to be a leader and deeply respected my parents' love-based values. My father was a colonel in the US Air Force, and my mother was a natural women's leader in ministry. As I met different influential leaders who saw potential on my life, I was grateful for the favor, and for who they were and their investment into me, but also disappointed by their driven, workaholic lives.

It sent me on a radical quest for balance, during which I discovered family really can be as fulfilling as your other purposes.

You can have healthy boundaries that lead to a healthy expression of self-significance. I spent years on this journey—both succeeding and failing at times—but I now lead an international ministry, do executive coaching, and have some best-selling books.

My wife and I get to revolve our lives around what God is doing and connect to that as a lifestyle. We have purposed in our hearts to tackle life with the goal of resting in his nature and letting that create a lifestyle of rest, peace, and patient perseverance. This requires a skill set that only comes when we actually develop it, and we want to master this way of life.

We're dreaming big dreams, taking risks, and keeping our hearts open so as to not miss a single thing God has for us and our children. Even now we are building our legacy, which is connecting people all over the world with the loving heart, mind, and goodness of God so they can do life in the fullness God designed for them.

www.bolzministries.com

NOTES

Notes

YOUR PERSONALITY 3

After taking the color.com test, I discovered that some of my strongest personal dislikes or turnoffs, which I thought were common sense no-nos for everyone, were actually specific to my personality type and not necessarily wrong or bad. Once I realized that, it was like a light came on. Though still annoying to me at times, for the most part, those things no longer hurt or offend me anymore when people do them.

~ Marcy B.

I'd always judged myself as being cold and hard because I didn't melt when a guy said he loved me. I appreciated it, but it didn't make my eyes roll back in my head in glee. I thought my girly girl gene was missing, but then I read about the five love languages and realized I felt loved through acts of service. I knew there wasn't anything wrong with me; I was just different.

~ Kimberly B.

I spent most of my life thinking there must be some seriously broken parts of my personality, because I was usually surrounded by people who thought and felt so differently about everything in life. I beat myself up a lot during that time for not being normal. Reading the Myers-Briggs test results was a lightbulb moment for me—I discovered there are other people similar to me in the world (but rare), and that I actually fit in as a part of a world mosaic.

~ Brenda S.

Seeing how my personality is shaped not only helped me understand myself, it also helped with parenting my children and getting along with other people close to me. It also helped me see the good things about my personality and not just the negative things.

~ Sharon B.

What I loved about the four temperaments results was that they gave me a basic understanding about others' strengths and weaknesses as well as my own. Even though I don't put people in a box, as all are uniquely different, it has still helped me understand how they are basically wired.

~ Yvonne B.

Of all the ways to figure out your place in this world, knowing your personality is one of the greatest aids to doing so. Say you're a woman who finds most people annoying, and you're always judging yourself because all you hear in your head is *That's not what normal women do. There must be something wrong with me.* Think back to everything you wrote in the first two chapters' exercise sections and come back to this question with a new perspective—one that says *I am the standard of normal for me. So what's right with me? How can I use that knowledge to make my life richer?*

There are many personality profile tests available that have changed lives, helping people become comfortable with their approaches to life and others, showing them careers they'd fit well into, and giving them better ways to communicate with those with other temperaments. The Myers-Briggs Type Indicator (MBTI), DISC, Personality Plus, Color Code, and 5 Love Languages are all recognized and worthwhile tests one can take. For most of them, the results will let you know which of four main categories you fall into when it comes to the way you work, act around others, and your perspective. Then it will show you exactly what kind of a mix you are in all those categories so you can see the kind of unique makeup you have—one no one else can match perfectly.

In one body we have many members, and the members do not all have the same function. ~ Romans 12:4

Obviously no profile assessment is perfect, because it fails to factor in the characteristics and habits you've inherited through your family line, especially from your parents. It also fails to include behaviors chosen because of the environment you've grown up in. The more introspective types could probably put a decent assessment of themselves together without the need of someone else's quiz, but there's always value in benefiting from the wisdom and experience of those who have put the time into developing these tools.

Some would say that Christians shouldn't take these types of tests because they're not biblical, but if you think about every good and perfect thing coming from the Father, I would say that a test that helps you understand yourself and others comes from the Father too. One of the seven spirits of the Lord is understanding (Isaiah 11:2).

We can do some guesswork on many biblical characters' personality types. For instance, Ruth was very loyal, adaptable, and willing to let others lead. "Where you go I will go" (Ruth 1:16). Jonah was very black and white, very focused on justice, and opinionated. "God said to Jonah, 'Do you do well to be angry for the plant?' And he said, 'Yes, I do well to be angry, angry enough to die'" (Jonah 4:9). Esther was outspoken but tactful and appreciative of the wisdom of others—she chose to not reveal the whole problem to the king in front of his court (Esther 16). David was impulsive, bloodthirsty, and fond of confrontation (2 Samuel 11). If any of them had done a personality profile assessment, would they have made the same choices in life? Perhaps.

Perhaps David would have razed a few less towns and learned some good communication skills instead. After all, if Saul was throwing things at him, it's highly possible that it was because David had a problem using the word *why* when he was asked to change songs the first time. He probably could have used a few hours learning the five love languages.

One of the other great things about knowing your personality is you can see your strengths and weaknesses more clearly at work. You can then talk to your manager (if he or she is receptive to your suggestions) about exemplifying your strengths while letting others fill those spots on the team where you are weak. Some people have seen how their jobs are not a good fit for them at all and have been able to make the move to jobs they actually enjoy and are good at. Ephesians 4 talks a lot about each part doing its work. "If you spend your life trying to be good at everything, you will never be great at anything" (Tom Rath, *Strengths Based Leadership*). The child says I can do it all by myself, while the child of God is humble and ready to give and receive. By letting go of the things you're not so great at, you're actually blessing others at work and in the home by giving them the opportunities to do what they love.

It's as if you are given the opportunity to be a better version of yourself when you know where you fit. The frustration of trying to be someone you are not is gone. The happiness of being given the green light to be the person you have always been is wonderful. You have the freedom to know all the details about your personality and accept them as being integral to being the person you were designed to be. Every part of your life becomes easier because you've been given understanding and revelation about yourself.

I've taken a number of the tests I mentioned earlier, and they've all added to my understanding and self-awareness. Seeing my strengths and accepting my weaknesses made me aware of how perfectly God designed me for the things I've done over my life: my study patterns, ways of learning, methods of communication, leading, following, organizing, taking risks, delegating, work ethic, and more. All the strong, weak, and completely deficient areas of my personality combine to form the one and only Sally Hanan of the world. Well, there are three other Sally Hanans I found on Facebook, but you know....

ASSESSMENTS

The following assessment looks at the core of how you think, and there are no right or wrong answers. The thing that makes this assessment useful is the fact that it puts language to your thought processes, so be careful not to select an answer based on what you think you "should" be. The quiz was put together by the team at TypeinMind.com, a team of four geniuses when it comes to analyzing personality types and then helping people learn how to communicate with all the other types around them in a healthy way.

The first question might take the most thought, especially if you are in your forties or older. As you have grown and matured, you have most likely developed other parts of you that were weaker as a child and become more balanced as a result. Although you might have a variety of strengths, in this quiz I'd like you to think about what you prefer and value above the other options, not necessarily what you've put the most work into developing. The goal is to identify the core part of you that has always been a strong preference throughout your life.

Of the four, check the description you identify with most strongly. Everyone has elements of each of these, but think about what you find to consistently be your "core"—the part of you that everything else serves most of the time—especially when you are at your happiest and healthiest.

_A_ I like to explore intriguing ideas and connections. I can easily think about the abstract or theoretical. I am very oriented around possibility and like to think *What if?* I can get consumed by what I am thinking and forget what actually is. I'm constantly thinking of new possibilities and solutions. I feel very different from most people, and I can think outside the box very easily. I think of so many possibilities that it can get overwhelming at times, and it frustrates me that I am unable to do all the things I can think of.

_B_ I'm fairly practical and sensible, and I learn best from experience. Overall, I lean more toward realism than airy fairy hopes and dreams. If I have a good idea, I want to get started on it fairly quickly, whether that's by doing the first step or creating a plan. I get frustrated if I'm expected to implement a poorly thought-out idea. It's easy for me to tell when someone's idea is impractical and not going to work in the real world.

_C_ I have a very high value for people and have strong personal beliefs. I feel like I'm really good at understanding people and their feelings. The decisions I make need to be aligned with who I am and what I believe in to sit right with me. I get frustrated when people are overly critical and don't realize how they're affecting people.

_D_ The facts, the data, and the truth are important to me. I spend a lot of time thinking about what is logical, efficient, and accurate. I like learning new information, and I enjoy coming up with optimal solutions to problems. I don't spend as much time focusing on feelings as others, and I hate the idea of emotionalism clouding my judgment. I struggle to relate to people who choose feelings over facts, especially if it is done at the expense of actually solving a problem or making a wise decision.

Once chosen, go to the following website page and enter that answer to get the next question: https://goo.gl/8gSkoZ. Apologies to anyone who does not have internet access—each question in the test is based on the previous question's answer, so it's too complicated a process to write all the section in this book. The quiz will bring you to your results, followed by both a short and long-term description of your personality type and how it operates. Your result will be fine-tuned as one unique type among many.

> *There's such a lot of different Annes in me. I sometimes think that is why I'm such a troublesome person. If I was just the one Anne, it would be ever so much more comfortable, but then it wouldn't be half so interesting.* ~ L.M. Montgomery, Anne of Green Gables

DISC PROFILES

For the sake of succinctness, I've put my summary of the DISC personality types (another assessment I mentioned) below so you can recognize each basic type and laugh a little at why Jesus focused so much on love. He knew just how irritating interesting people could be.

The DISC assessment puts you into one main category and then adds on particular traits from other types to give you your final unique personality type. In the table below, you'll find you are mostly or veering toward one type with a small or large mix of one or two others, so your final result will be Id, or Sc, etc. The gray bars around the four boxes of types are those traits two types share.

	ASSERTIVE, BOLD, FAST-PACED, OUTSPOKEN, ACTIVE	
D - DRIVE - WHAT		**I - INFLUENCE - WHO**
Sees the big picture		Shows enthusiasm, optimistic
Gets results		Open and approachable
Gets straight to the point		Persuasive
Firm		Friendly, outgoing
Driven, sense of urgency		Good verbal skills, talkative
Assertive, direct		Encouraging
Change agent		Shows confidence
Fixes problems		High trust in others
C - CONSCIENTIOUSNESS - WHY		**S - STEADINESS - HOW**
Has objective reasoning skills		Has a calm manner & approach
Cautious		Responsible
Values excellence, precision		Supportive
Enjoys details		Sincere
Likes procedures		Adaptable, accommodating
Reserved		Relational, amiable
Objective		Persistent
Analytical		Good listener
Not talkative		Patient

Left side: LOGICAL, QUESTIONING, TASK ORIENTED, DISCIPLINED, FOCUSED
Right side: AGREEABLE, WARM, ACCEPTING, PEOPLE FOCUSED, RECEPTIVE
Bottom: PASSIVE, CAREFUL, REFLECTIVE, CALM, RELIABLE

YOUR PERSONALITY

The beautiful part of all this, as I've mentioned, is in the value it adds to your expectations. For example, let's say I want a cake baked for my daughter's twenty-first birthday.

If I ask the I to make it, she'll get totally razzed up about the idea of the cake—colors, design, height. She'll ask me about my daughter and persuade me to go with the cake vision she has in her head rather than the one I have in mine. She'll appear totally confident in her abilities to do it and won't even ask about a deadline. However, she might never follow through. Other, more exciting things might turn up that distract her. She might forget she has to make the cake at all, and we're all upset we ever chose her in the first place. She might then feel bad about it for the rest of her life and apologize about it every time she meets me.

If I ask the D to make it, he'll look at me as if I have three heads and immediately tell me no, he won't make the cake. He's too busy, for one, not to mention he's not interested in doing it and there are other, better bakers he knows who can do the job perfectly; would I like him to call the bakery right now?

If I ask the S to make it, he'll bend over backward to accommodate me, giving up every single minute of his free time to make sure I get the cake of my dreams. Not only will he follow my list to the letter, he'll deliver it on time and be very open to any last-minute changes I might want to make to the design. Nothing is too much trouble for the S, because he wants me to be happy with his work.

If I ask the C to make it, she'll ask me why I want that particular design, that flavor, those colors. It would be so much better if it was a blue cake with an airplane, because that's just what good cakes look like these days. I'll need to give her a month's advance notice, plus a deadline, so she can make sure every detail is followed to the letter. She'll make me sign a contract in advance to make sure I don't change any of the directions, and she'll try to keep all messages to texts or e-mails so she can eliminate our social communication as much as possible. I will receive an absolutely perfect cake on time.

It does us good to laugh at ourselves. We're all irritating at times, and that's okay.

Everybody you know has a story in his or her head of who you are, including yourself. But God has a story in his head about you too, and you get to decide whose story you're going to pay attention to.

FINISH THESE SENTENCES

Now that I've read the results, I'm willing/not willing to accept that this is the personality type I have because

My understanding of the results makes me think/feel

When I look back at the choices I've made in the past with the current knowledge of my personality type, I

When I look at all the relationships I currently have—family, friends, work—I can see that a person with my personality type can

When I look at others I interact with regularly, I can see how I can communicate with them in the following ways, based on their personality types:

TRUTH

What is the truth about your unique personality? Mull over the following Scriptures and write down anything God shows you through them.

"We, though many, are one body in Christ, and individually members one of another." (Romans 12:5)

"God arranged the members in the body, each one of them, as he chose." (1 Corinthians 12:18)

"Every good gift and every perfect gift is from above, coming down from the Father of lights with whom there is no variation or shadow due to change." (James 1:17)

"For the body does not consist of one member but of many. ... If the whole body were an eye, where would be the sense of hearing? If the whole body were an ear, where would be the sense of smell?" (1 Corinthians 12:14–18)

GLENN'S JOURNEY (MID-FIFTIES)

It was a dark and stormy night when I realized being afraid of the dark was cliché and common, but being convinced that darkness invited spiders to an observe-and-report position made me a friend of a single sixty-watt, frosted bulb in the center of my bedroom. It was from this place that my imagination gave voice to a yellow horse with a bladder condition, an alter ego named Roy, and stories long since forgotten.

Growing up in Wyoming, my parents were less cheerleaders and more believers. If I wanted to try something new, I should try it and see if it could be done. No pom-poms required. I often thought of this as a liability. My friends weren't much of the pom-pom type either. Knowing my place was important—and less humiliating. What my dad taught me, in his own way, is that if I waited to ask permission for every dream I encountered, I'd probably be stuck in neutral drifting back down a hill I really wanted to climb.

I was fairly confident and took to new tasks easily and with a great desire to learn. The idea of freedom to fail was important to me. From the age of fourteen on, I worked a variety of jobs, and the execution of those jobs helped me learn what I could do easily and what would require more skills training. I made my way through lawn care, food service, and farming before I made my way to the local skating rink, where I began to understand some of my skills, and where I would eventually meet my wife.

Support became a personal need when I purchased my first home at nineteen. My family were pretty clear they still liked me, but they didn't offer to pay rent, buy groceries, or cuddle me on stormy nights. It didn't seem to bother me, and I found it had been a long time since I needed light to keep a SWAT team of spiders from taking me captive.

In my early twenties I moved from being a disc jockey at the local skating rink to an on-air personality at the local radio station. I spent four and a half years being moved from one department to another and holding titles for almost every position they had. I like wearing lots of hats and learning everything I can. That has led to a career in broadcasting that is well in excess of three decades.

It was in the year my daughter was born that I added professional writer to my list of credits. I had written thousands of commercials for radio clients, and that creative writing led easily to other types of writing. A friend and I started writing for a good news publication (still in production more than twenty years later). I eventually became editor, then passed the role on when I was called to a new ministry. My first book was published in 1999, and I have either written or contributed to more than 120 books since then.

I don't believe you have to be inspired to write. I believe you just need to sit down and write. Writing is work. As it turns out, editors seem to like it when a writer can write to a deadline, stay inside the word count, and complete assignments. I used to have an advice column for writers, and it was always fun to see how some of the practical ideas I shared resulted in contracts and published writing. So to recap, while pom-poms were not a part of my past, I am a firm believer that I should shake them on behalf of others.

If you do it right, you can live a long life; and if you ever get to the place where you think you've learned it all, then even with the continuation of heartbeats, your purpose for living may need to be resuscitated.

I have taken college classes with no college credit simply because it was a subject I wanted to know more about. I've hung out with people who have skills I wanted to learn. I have been willing to share whatever it is I know. I contacted an editor after having a submission rejected and asked if he could help me understand where I went wrong. I think he had his own pom-poms, because he responded by giving me advice and a chance to rewrite the content, which, after a second rejection, resulted in an offer to write five to seven modules per book for all thirty-plus volumes.

I learned to refuse to give up easily, never think my lack of success is someone else's fault, and never allow others to determine who I will become. The last time I checked, God's got a plan and he keeps calling me forward. Grace gives me freedom beyond failure.

My wife considers me a steady Eddie. I'm even keeled and believe that life is more about the choices we make than the feelings we feel. Maybe I'm just a few degrees away from normal. I grew up a nonconformist, and that trend shows no signs of slowing. I am comfortable in my skin, generally pleased with my life choices, love my family, and I just don't feel the need to impress people. There are many people in my circle of friendships who have no idea I am an author, and I don't do anything to change their lack of knowledge.

We each have our story, and we may believe ours is either the best or worst. It's not; it's just a story, and every nuance is part of what makes you *you*. Your story has the ability to connect with some and not with others. It can be encouraging or a cautionary tale. Embrace what you've lived through—your story is important. Maybe you hadn't noticed, but every story in the Bible describes someone who is uniquely different from anyone else.

If you understand your purpose, then do what you need to do. I'll be standing on my side of the screen with virtual pom-poms flashing in the glow of my sixty-watt lightbulb.

www. kjil991.com/glenn-hascall

Notes

Notes

WHAT YOU DO

Gifts + Talents

I'm a real nut for organization and efficiency. I decided many years ago that I did not want to spend my life chasing my tail. Also, these traits were good to have in the workplace. Now that I'm in poor health, it's so helpful. I live alone, and I seriously am not well enough to do things any other way. I couldn't see how valuable these traits would be to me, but God could when he made me this way. I'm grateful.

~ Laurie G.

I think there are two types of gifts. The first one is a gift God gives us to change the world or to change the lives of those around us—or indeed, to change our own lives by drawing us closer to him. The other is a gift God gives us simply for our delight. I believe wholeheartedly that it delights him to delight us with gifts in which we delight. And maybe that's what my passions are for me—simple delight.

~ Sarah M.

I am pretty creative when I sense a call from the Lord. I have written prose and poetry, drawn, painted, and composed music.

~ Judith R.

I've always had a good voice, stamina, compassion, empathy, and a passion for pregnancy and birth. As an adult, I realized that all of those gifts and talents were great for being a doula, which I love! Ironically, though, he revealed this as my gift and then asked me to put it away for a season while I was raising my kids. However, he told me I would get to use it again one day, and he has been faithful with that promise.

~ Sharon O.

I've always had an intuitive connection with animals, particularly dogs, which then led me to work with dogs. I now own a dog training center and have been able to help thousands of dog owners, of all ages, have a better relationship with their best friends.

~ Diana S.

Talent, gift, ability, strength—it's something you have a knack for. It comes easily to you; you're naturally good at it. It doesn't necessarily mean you enjoy it, but for some God-known reason, it's an inherent part of you.

> *The trick to creativity, if there is a single useful thing to say about it, is to identify your own peculiar talent and then settle down to work with it for a good long time. The trick is to recognize it, to honor it, to work with it. This is where creativity starts . . . the cultivation of aptitude, far more than coincidence or inspiration, is responsible for most creative breakthroughs.* ~ Denise Shekerjian

Knowing what you're good at naturally ties in with knowing the strengths and weaknesses of your personality mix. The more you know, the better choices you can make in the jobs you go for and in the education you pursue. You can see where you fit before even traveling that way. If all teenagers understood and appreciated their personalities and interests, I don't think we'd be seeing the huge number of dropouts and changes of majors we do. The money saved would be astronomical. CEOs of the best companies in the world know that the best way to grow their companies and keep employees is through discovering, championing, developing, and utilizing the talent within their ranks. They call it human capital, because they know that it's one of their biggest assets.

Many of the lesser-known biblical characters had convenient talents that quite possibly saved lives and blessed many. For instance,

Jael had great hammering skills. (Judges 4:17–22; 5:6, 24–27)

Samson was no pushover ... unless you cut his hair off. (Judges 13–16).

Ehud was a smooth talker. (Judges 3:14–30).

Jethro was strategic. (Exodus 18).

Shamgar had serious weaponry skills. (Judges 3:31)

Jabez knew how to use a few words to gain much. (Chronicles 4:10)

Rahab automatically discerned the winning side. (Joshua 2: 6)

Your gifts and talents could have already saved lives and blessed others, or maybe they've only saved your own life and blessed you so far, but you've got time. Although every time I try to diagnose my health on WebMD, I have a little less faith in that statement.

*The two most important days in your life are the day you were born
and the day you find out why. ~ Anonymous*

Many of us have been taught that we should never show off our gifts, that doing so is bragging and that's one of the seven deadly sins, or eighth, maybe. But how on earth would anything get done if no one knew what we were good at?

All over the world, in every area of life, people have spaces that need to be filled. And how will they know to ask you to fill one unless you've revealed all of you? Take any job interview. You put your resume together and list all your talents, skills, and past employment specifically so the future employer can see if you fill the need he or she has. How will you shine like a city on a hill unless you turn on the light?

If you shut down and hide your talent because you're afraid that to use it would be showing off, you're effectively telling God that even though he gave you something wonderful, you don't think much of it and would rather hide it away to keep it safe, away from people who can sully it with their judgments about it. There's a little story in the Bible about that—about the guy who buried his talent in the ground so no one would rob it. He didn't put it in the bank so it could get its 0.02 percent. He didn't invest it in a business venture. He dug a hole in the ground and let it sit there because he was afraid. The very thing of value he had been gifted with, a gift that could enrich his life and show off his boss in the best light, was seen through his eyes as a curse and thrown into darkness like a useless lump of clay.

This world needs all of you, everything you are made up of, to show up and participate. Treat life like a job interview—find out where you can bring life and show up. You don't have to show off, but don't hide any of your talents. Whether your gifts are creative, intellectual, physical, or intuitive, there's a place for them to be used to bless others.

Life is not a musical, although it would probably be more fun if it were, but even a good musical needs about two hundred talented people to pull it off—set designers and artists, performing artists, light technicians, camera technicians, sound operators, tailors, scriptwriters, a director, and more. Life needs you in all your weirdness and funky freshness. It needs teams of people to show up and do their unique things. And it's good practice ... what else did you think was on the list for the entertainment at the wedding feast?

ASSESSMENT

Mark each item below with one of the following scores based on how good you are at it naturally, as in, it's a natural talent rather than a learned skill:

5 = High (top 10 percent of my age group), 4 = Above average (upper 25 percent), 2 = Below average (lower 25 percent), 1 = Low (bottom 10 percent).

__ Working with my hands—having manual dexterity, coordinated

__ Working with machines and tools—building and fixing mechanical things

__ Solving problems and puzzles

__ Working with computers

__ Helping people solve problems—diagnostic reasoning that connects the dots and sizes up situations quickly

__ Helping people feel better—putting them at ease, being kind

__ Teaching people how to do things

__ Leading projects and people—providing direction, motivating, presenting ideas

__ Selling things or ideas—able to persuade, bargain, influence

__ Working with number—understanding formulas and word problems, doing mental math quickly

__ Working with science—applying systematic problem solving and reasoning to biology, physics, and chemistry

__ Being organized—keeping track, following a schedule, being systematic

__ Having analytical reasoning—catching errors, fact-checking, reaching conclusions by analyzing data

__ Learning about history and geography

__ Caring for family and home—serving tactfully and patiently with love

__ Understanding industrial technology

__ Able to organize thoughts and communicate them easily through writing or speaking

__ Having spatial perception—seeing an object like a map or blueprint in the mind from every angle

THINK IT THROUGH, FIGURE IT OUT

Circle and write your top three talents below for use in a later exercise.

1.
2.
3.

Which of your higher scored talents are abilities you've let die because you have no interest in using them?

How do you feel about letting them die?

Which of your higher scored talents are abilities you've spent time developing because you enjoyed using them?

How do you feel about giving them life?

"The great ages did not perhaps produce much more talent than ours,'" [T.S.] Eliot wrote. "But less talent was wasted."
~ *Jonah Lehrer,* Imagine: How Creativity Works

FINISH THESE SENTENCES

I think natural talent is

I am/am not okay with letting others know about my talents because

I would love to develop my natural talents and abilities because

I think I might have downplayed or ignored my talents in the past because

For the next few days I'm going to start paying more attention to what comes naturally to me, like

TRUTH

What is the truth about your talents? Mull over the following Scriptures and write down anything God shows you through them.

> "For it will be like a man going on a journey, who called his servants and entrusted to them his property. To one he gave five talents, to another two, to another one, to each according to his ability. Then he went away. He who had received the five talents went at once and traded with them, and he made five talents more. So also he who had the two talents made two talents more. But he who had received the one talent went and dug in the ground and hid his master's money." (Matthew 25:14–30)

> "Pray for us, for we are sure that we have a clear conscience, desiring to act honorably in all things." (Hebrews 13:18)

> "I have [plans] for you, ... plans for welfare and not for evil." (Jeremiah 29:11)

JANE'S JOURNEY (EARLY FIFTIES)

I was born and raised in Canada and had a great childhood. I was the only girl of five children, and by the time I was born, my parents were older and wiser. My dad spent a lot of time encouraging us all, and he had a lot of wisdom to share, which I loved listening to. I never felt limited—we could do anything, and independence was encouraged.

I loved science and French in school; it gave me a background to the world God created. I pursued knowledge and strengthened my faith by studying the Bible a lot. I was shy around others and had mild dyslexia, which made reading difficult, but it didn't stop me. We were part of a community-oriented church. It was a safe place to be and the teaching was always good. I knew my Bible inside-out because of it, and I knew how strong my relationship with God was.

I started working for my dad when I was fourteen and earned enough to buy my own clothes and things I needed for school. I did a little of everything at the warehouse—cleaning floors, repackaging items, processing orders, shipping, and keeping the basement organized. My dad had been in business since I was four and working for him was an education in itself on the ins and outs of owning a small business. I saw the value of hard work. Although my dad was never able to take a vacation, between him and Mom (who had a job outside the home), they provided for us well.

I traveled to France as a foreign exchange student as a teenager and went to university there. It was meant to be for ten months, but I got terribly homesick and came home after six. I don't regret leaving early, because I know I wasn't emotionally equipped to handle it. Some of the people in the house were not fond of the mention of God, and the spiritual warfare was draining.

I put myself through college and graduated without debt. Most of my time there was spent either studying or working, so I never saw it as a social experiment. A few years later I got married and moved to Texas, where we raised our three kids. While everyone has regrets about the things they didn't do with their kids, I feel that we did what we could with what we knew and God took care of the rest. We were able to serve in three different churches over the years, and we learned a lot from each place—things we have been able to either carry forward or tuck away as an experience we'd rather not repeat. Even in that, though, God has been so good about teaching us how to apply his perspective of love to every situation.

Looking back over it all, I can see how life is an amazing journey. These days I see myself as a person who is actively moving forward and there for anyone who wants prayer support, encouragement, or advice. I have a part-time job at my church, so my time is flexible enough to be there for my husband and the kids when needed. Now that all the kids have either graduated or are in college, we're facing a new crossroads that includes a lot of freedom. After all these years of my husband carrying the load, it's exciting to be able to plan for the rest of our lives together.

I've gained a lot of wisdom over the years and invested in lives that have borne fruit. I have a daily opportunity to choose joy and to speak life into everything I face, and that's what I'm learning how to do these days. It can be hard at times, with our children far from home going through their own life circumstances, but I take a long-term look at everything. I get to cast vision with them for the future, and every decision they make today is a life decision that can affect their generation. I want my children to do what God's called them to do in their realms of influence, release the righteousness of the kingdom into their communities, and bring freedom. This is not the job of one person; it's up to every individual to release freedom to his or her arena. One word can change everything, and faithfulness can change the course of history. And that's what I want my legacy to be—to be known as one who was faithful and who spoke life and freedom into the places and hearts where she had influence.

> *Go placidly amid the noise and the haste, and remember what peace there may be in silence. As far as possible without surrender, be on good terms with all persons. Speak your truth quietly and clearly, and listen to others, even the dull and ignorant; they too have their story. Be yourself. Especially do not feign affection. Neither be cynical about love—for in the face of all aridity and disenchantment it is perennial as the grass. Take kindly the counsel of the years, gracefully surrendering the things of youth. Nurture strength of spirit to shield you from misfortune. But do not distress yourself with imaginings. Many fears are born of fatigue and loneliness. Beyond a wholesome discipline, be gentle with yourself. You are a child of the universe no less than the trees and the stars; you have a right to be here. And whether or not it is clear to you, no doubt the universe is unfolding as it should. Therefore be at peace with God, whatever you conceive Him to be, and whatever your labours and aspirations, in the noisy confusion of life keep peace with your soul. With all its sham, drudgery and broken dreams, it is still a beautiful world.*
> ~ *Max Ehrmann,* Desiderata: A Poem for a Way of Life

Notes

GIFTS + TALENTS

Notes

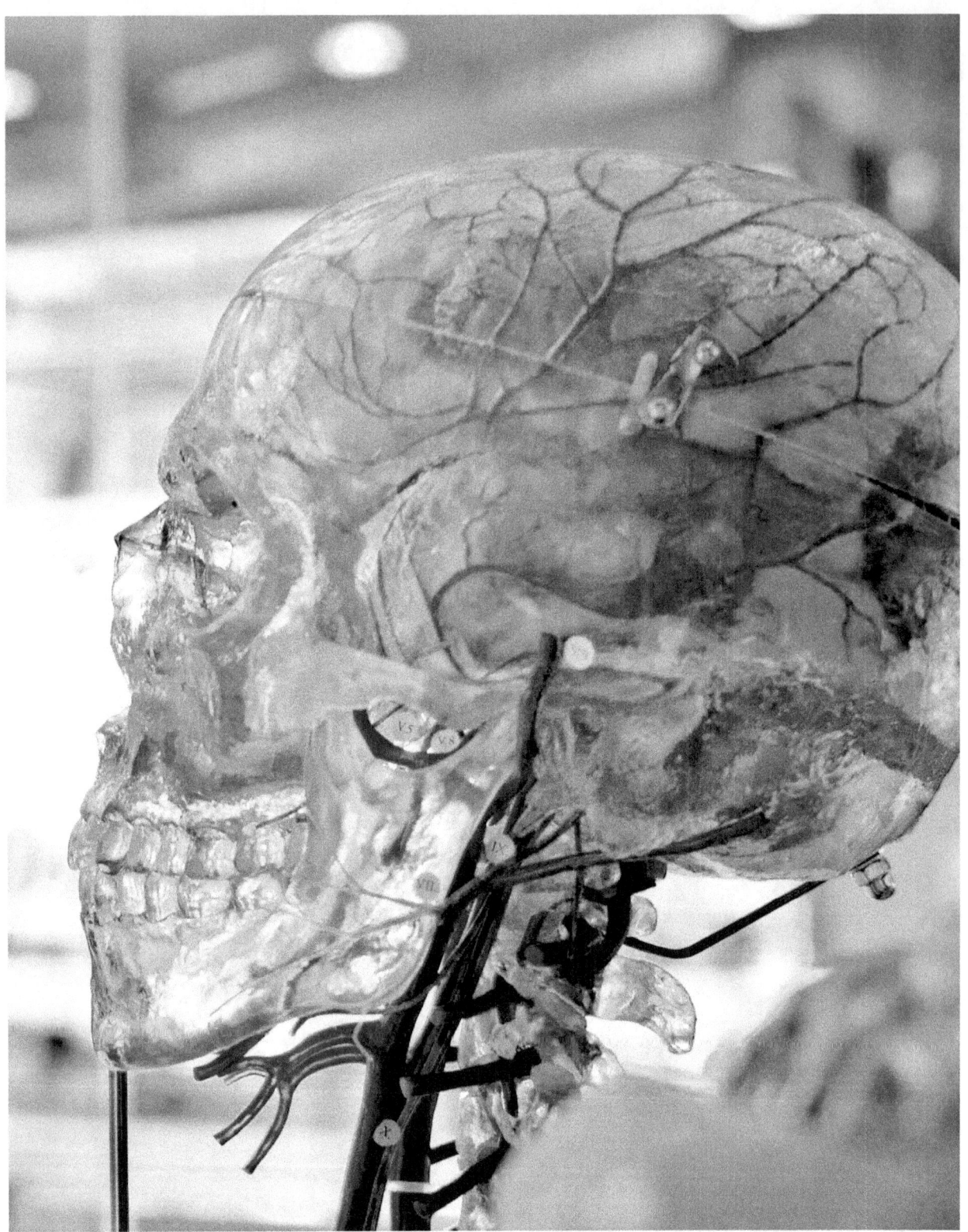

KNOWLEDGE + EXPERIENCE 5

I learned how to draw in school and thought I'd never use it again, but first I used it in my home schooling, and then I kept expanding it to add more and more media. Then I started teaching classes at our local rec center. Then I taught private lessons. Next, when I went back to teaching full time, I took the certification test and did well! I do not have any formal art education, but the certification did look good on my résumé as I searched for my English teaching job. Finally, last summer, I wrote and illustrated a book for one of my grandsons ... and then one for his brother. Then someone hired me to illustrate hers. I am not wildly successful at this point, but I am having a grand time. I always felt certain I would write when I retired from teaching. Now I can see art also being a big part of the equation.

~ Kristi F.

As an artist, I always feel like I was born to get lost in the moment ... but now I'm a business owner and that doesn't really work. Learning basic time management skills has helped me manage my resources well.

~ Page V.

I was always daydreaming and storytelling (quite intertwined for me). I was forever getting in trouble for talking in school and "making up outlandish things," according to some. It wasn't until Mrs. Unger (twelfth-grade creative writing teacher) recognized my abilities that I even began to consider that storytelling was a gift. Now I can call it world building, character development, plot hatching, and all the other elements that go into writing fiction.

~ Miles O.

I learned typing from a manual in high school to then learning how to use all the word processors and beyond. I worked as a legal secretary for years and then went into admin stuff. Now no one needs the worker of the past, but I have so much knowledge pre-technology that is still needed today. And maybe us geezers will have a place some day. I'm seventy-four and working full time still. Typing is so much a part of my provision, thanks to that manual.

~ Karen T.

We often find that the more experience and knowledge we acquire on any subject or skill set, the less our natural talents seem to matter. The years of fine-tuning any talent pay off to where we are useful, contributing members of society. Because what use is talent unless you learn how to use it?

Malcolm Gladwell, in his stunning book *Outliers: The Story of Success,* says, "Achievement is talent plus preparation," and "Researchers have settled on what they believe is the magic number for true expertise: ten thousand hours." In other words, all the talent in the world can't match the expertise you gain through practice.

But what about looking at that the other way around: Can you be really good at something if you start out with no talent at all? Possibly. It depends on the skill you want to develop. Writers can write for that length of time and learn all the rules and write lovely books, but they might still miss causing that *thump thump* of the heart the reader gets from exquisite writing. But think of all the books you've read that didn't necessarily have the magic but still fed your heart. Aren't you glad those writers put the effort into developing their craft, that those doctors interned, that those violin makers kept carving and sanding?

Working really hard is what successful people do.
~ Malcolm Gladwell, Outliers: The Story of Success

When you combine natural talent with practice, you have the winning strategy for maximizing what you were born with. Ten thousand hours is a long time. It's close to five years of practicing for forty hours every week. Yes, the thought can make you want to give up already. But hold on there. How many jobs have you held for five years? How many times have you used and developed an innate skill in a job, learning skills because the job required it and you became good at them? Exactly. Life has been giving you knowledge and experience all along, and God will make sure none of it is wasted.

As I've mentioned in my workbook *Empower Yourself,* I got a nursing degree, but I was a terrible nurse. But, but ... I can hear all you empaths trying to reassure me already. Trust me. All my fellow nurses agreed, because I couldn't multitask, and that's one of the main requirements to being a good nurse. There are always ten things going on at once and you can't neglect any of them. But there were so many things I can look back on that I know I did well. I was great at encouraging scared patients, at explaining what the setup would be like when they came out of surgery, at cheering them up, at explaining to visitors what to expect before letting them go in to see their relatives. I was able to take those skills and use them later in life to teach and counsel. And even later in life, I was able to translate those skills into words and put them into books. Nothing is wasted.

God knows what he's doing. Even if you're working in what you'd call a dead-end job right now, you're learning invaluable skills. I drove for ridesharing companies for two years of my forties, and that job was a gift, because not only did I get to help pay bills after decades of raising kids as a stay-at-home mom and calling all the shots, I also finally learned how to offer excellent service to every personality type. Everything you do is an opportunity for learning, which will, in turn, benefit others. (My husband is still benefiting.)

Moses spent forty years learning how to be a good shepherd, a skill he needed badly in order to round up those Israeli "sheep" during all their dithering about whether to stay in Egypt or go. Not only that, but he learned many things from his father-in-law about leadership. It was Jethro who advised him to delegate others to judge the smaller matters of the Israelites so he wouldn't wear himself out. Moses was still learning and developing his gifts even after leading his people out of Egypt (Exodus 18).

When we need something done, we hire a professional to do it if we know we don't have the skills needed to do it ourselves. Who would hire a singer to remodel a kitchen, or a financial advisor to edit a book, or a teacher to star in a blockbuster movie? No one. We need everyone to function in his or her gifts. We often attach more value to the spiritual gifts of the Spirit than to the natural gifts, but they are all gifts. They are all spiritual, because we were crafted by the Spirit. Why would we insult God by valuing one aspect of his gifts over others?

God is highly practical, as evidenced by the detail with which he planned the world's systems of nature, food production, human interaction, and industry. His desire to bring solutions through practical means is evident everywhere, and we get to be the ones who make it all happen! Not only are we all necessary cogs in all the wheels of life, but we are also vital. We need to be skilled though. We need to bring our best, give our best, do our best. We need to develop everything we have in responsible ways to steward our experience and knowledge and turn them all into ways to bless others. We are God's human capital—his beloved, talented family ready to invest and produce fruit wherever we are established.

Hard work is a prison sentence only if it does not have meaning. Once it does, it becomes the kind of thing that makes you grab your wife around the waist and dance a jig.
   ~ Malcolm Gladwell, Outliers; The Story of Success

ASSESSMENT

Mark each item with one of the following scores based on how good you are at it because you've learned it, as in, it's an acquired skill rather than a natural talent:

5 = High (top 10 percent of my age group), 4 = Above average (upper 25 percent), 2 = Below average (lower 25 percent), 1 = Low (bottom 10 percent).

__ Working with my hands—having manual dexterity, coordinated

__ Working with machines and tools—building and fixing mechanical things

__ Solving problems and puzzles

__ Working with computers

__ Helping people solve problems—diagnostic reasoning that connects the dots and sizes up situations quickly

__ Helping people feel better—putting them at ease, being kind

__ Teaching people how to do things

__ Leading projects and people—providing direction, motivating, presenting ideas

__ Selling things or ideas—able to persuade, bargain, influence

__ Working with numbers—understanding formulas and word problems, doing mental math quickly

__ Working with science—applying systematic problem solving and reasoning to biology, physics, and chemistry

__ Being organized—keeping track, following a schedule, being systemic

__ Having analytical reasoning—catching errors, fact checking, reaching conclusions by analyzing data

__ Learning about history and geography

__ Caring for family and home—serving tactfully and patiently with love

__ Understanding industrial technology

__ Able to organize thoughts and communicate them easily through writing or speaking

__ Having spatial perception—seeing an object like a map or blueprint in the mind from every angle

THINK IT THROUGH, WORK IT OUT

Circle and write your top three learned skills below for use in a later exercise.

1.
2.
3.

Which of your higher scored learned skills are abilities you've let die because you have no interest in using them?

How do you feel about letting them die?

Which of your higher scored learned skills are abilities you've spent time developing because you enjoyed using them?

How do you feel about having given them life?

The Christian gospel is a two-way road. On the one hand, it seeks to change the souls of men, and thereby unite them with God; on the other hand, it seeks to change the environmental conditions of men so the soul will have a chance after it is changed.
~ Martin Luther King, Jr.

FINISH THESE SENTENCES

I think the skills I've acquired are

I'm open/not open to using my acquired or developed skills because

I'm open/not open to asking those I know what skills they're hiding because

I would love/not love to develop my skills from their current level because

When I think about demonstrating my skills to people who don't even know I have them, I

For the next few days, I'm going to start

TRUTH

What is the truth about developing your skills? Mull over the following Scriptures and write down anything God shows you through them.

"Do you see a man skilled in his work? He will serve before kings; he will not serve before obscure men." (Proverbs 22:29)

"When I saw, I reflected upon it; I looked, and received instruction." (Proverbs 24:32)

"For land that has drunk the rain that often falls on it, and produces a crop useful to those for whose sake it is cultivated, receives a blessing from God. But if it bears thorns and thistles, it is worthless and near to being cursed, and its end is to be burned." (Proverbs 4:1–4)

"Whatever your hand finds to do, do it with your might." (Ecclesiastes 9:10)

"And let steadfastness have its full effect, that you may be perfect and complete, lacking in nothing." (James 1:2–4)

STEPHEN'S JOURNEY (EARLY THIRTIES)

My dad encouraged me a lot growing up, especially in my love of music. My mom was a bit more of a truth teller and didn't want to give me false hope. You could always find me at worship gatherings during high school—that's where I felt the happiest. Music reached me in ways nothing else could. I also loved reading because it fed my thirst for learning, and I found history and geography captivating.

I was good at following rules even though I didn't appreciate authority, but my parents kept me very sheltered, which made me very afraid of normal social interaction. Other kids made fun of me, and I didn't have the communication skills or social intelligence I needed to defend myself. On top of that, my parents divorced, and I got very angry. I had to change schools. Life was too hard without my dad around, but thanks to the way my parents had raised me, I never went completely crazy … or I was never brave enough to. And then God won me over and I surrendered.

Once out of high school, I had no idea what I wanted to do, and my lack of self-confidence made my indecision even worse. Even finishing high school had been a struggle. I didn't know how to study, and I didn't want to work; I just wanted to do music ministry. I'd spent two years working as a busboy, followed by a year at a building supply store and a few months at a fast food restaurant, but I wasn't happy. To be honest, I'd based my work ethic on my personal happiness and felt a little entitled.

My dad got fed up with my attitude and kicked me out, even though he knew I hadn't enough life skills to survive on my own. My mother refused to take me in as well. It took me years to get over that rejection. I tried working in sales, at a call center, and as a delivery guy. Some jobs let you know what you never want to do again.

Then I got engaged and I knew things had to change. I'd always been interested in the medical field, so I got into an EMT program but couldn't handle the study and used up all my retakes on the final test. After that crushing disappointment, I managed to graduate from the Fire Department, only to find it would take at least two to three years to get a job with them.

I was sick and tired of everything, and to top it all, my local church added to the pain. I was overwhelmed and hurting and ran to another state to take a job I never should have taken, leaving my wife back home. I only lasted four months in that job, and by the end of it I was drinking a lot and letting my mind entertain a lot of things I hadn't allowed in before. Medical issues were flaring up from the stress of it all. My wife moved to join me but felt isolated, and then she became severely depressed after her best friend died unexpectedly. We had no support system in place because we weren't part of a church there and had left all our friends behind.

We finally moved back home. I began working as an ICU and floating tech at a nearby hospital while also beginning nursing training. My wife began to recover, as did I. We're doing well, although the one thing that aches the most these days is the lack of a child, despite our many efforts to realize that dream. We've become stronger for it all, and part of that is because we were and are willing to grow together. We're on the way to where we're going.

I'm called to heal. I've experienced brokenness and healing myself, and I know what family looks like. I can bring hope and health into other people's lives. I'm hungry to find better ways of bringing healing about and doing things well. There's always room for improvement. I feel valued in this place. My relationships are good, and I feel I'm making good use of my time. I think I'm about 95 percent comfortable with letting people see the real me, which is so different to how I felt in school. Healing wise, I'm at about 75 percent of where I could be to be whole, but that's okay. I'm still healing.

I will never stop loving worship, and lately I've been able to join our worship team and serve in that capacity, which probably ministers to me more than anyone else in the room. God knows.

At my age, I don't think I know all the reasons as to why I'm here at this time in history, but learning more, helping more, doing more will always be my mantra. What I've discovered is that I only ever want God to be my center. There's no earthly substance I want to pull an eternal reality out of, and I hope to live the rest of my life from that perspective and leave it as my legacy.

In a world where everyone demands respect and entitlement by asking, "Don't you know who I am?" Jesus, the one deserving the most honor, instead asks, "Who do you say that I am?" It was more important to him that people see him for themselves, instead of him having to promote and push his royalty as some sort of valuable status symbol they should worship (even though it was just that). Real humility requires confidence in who God made you to be.
~ Carla Pratico

Notes

Notes

SPIRITUAL GIFTS

6

The outcome of discovering a spiritual gift depends on our response to that discovery. When I realized that I was prophetic, I developed a confidence that started a process of moving me out of my own insecurities and into a world of being a contribution to those around me. That, in turn, started fulfilling the real desires of my heart.

~ Jason S.

I never really wanted to lead or felt like I was good at it, but from a young age I kept being put in leadership type positions. Now I desire to become a good leader, and I feel like it was a gift of mine all along, I just didn't realize it until recently.

~Aspen B.

I was born with a few things I could either call an interest or a spiritual gift. Sometimes I'll feel like sparkly Jell-O after counseling, doing inner healing work, speaking, writing, or giving, whereas even thinking about a gift like administration or martyrdom would make me want to go take a nap. Some gifts I seem to drop in and out of, like speaking wisdom, whereas others are fed by spending time in certain environments or by learning more through information and practice. Ultimately, the more time I spend in God's presence, the more I seem ready to flow in when it's needed. Maybe it's because all my receptors are on, whereas when I don't hang out with the one who makes me whole, I'm not open to letting him pass through.

~ Sally H.

My main spiritual gift is teaching. I get the most joy when students tell me they learned something new that they'll be able to use.

~ Kristen S.

There are two gifts in particular that I downplayed and questioned for years due to a negative self-image and lack of confidence. Once I accepted that the gifts of writing and hearing the voice of God were real, I was able to step out of my comfort zone, which has brought me the pleasure of seeing hearts and lives powerfully impacted and healed. Walking in those gifts has formed my perspective of myself and others into a life-giving force.

~ Traci V.

We cannot gain a full understanding of our makeup without looking at the spiritual gifts we have been given too. As I mentioned earlier, we can't give the gifts of the Spirit more value than the gifts we were given at conception, because they both come from the same source—a Father who knows exactly what he's doing with his generosity.

The following pages are filled with descriptions of what are commonly called the gifts of the Spirit. You'll notice that some of them overlap with personality types, natural talents, and learned skills, as they should. We should never categorize creation into distinct boxes when God is such a master at fusing each of us into a distinct person. As you read, mark the gifts you can identify as having.

I did not write this very thorough list. A young couple I have the pleasure of knowing put a lot of time and effort into it as part of a comprehensive spiritual gifts inventory. Remember their names—Rebecca and Nathan Alexander. You'll see a lot more of them in the years to come because Rebecca has a lot of revelatory insight and wisdom that the world needs, and Nathan is beautifully gifted in writing.

ADMINISTRATION

1 Corinthians 12:28; Acts 4:32–37 | This special ability is represented most commonly in those who possess the gift of leadership, but it is also found in those who are under the guidance of leaders (helpers). Administrators make good strategists and tend to be well equipped at handling the details of turning a vision into a reality; this often includes the direction and management of time, people, money, and other resources.

APOSTLESHIP

1 Corinthians 12:28; Romans 1:5 | This is a God-given responsibility to those who will be pioneers of the kingdom of God, leading others to extend the reach of influence. Apostles are gifted in overseeing the development of new churches or ministry structures.

CELIBACY

Matthew 19:10–12; 1 Corinthians 7:7 | The special ability God gives to some to voluntarily remain single without regret and maintain control over sexual impulses to serve the Lord without distraction. Those who have this gift remain single because they feel they can serve the Lord better that way.

COMMUNITY BUILDER

Hebrews 10:24–25; Acts 2:42–44 | Community builders are the networkers of God's kingdom. Warm and friendly, they are vitally important at helping visitors and new members feel welcome and get plugged into the community. They are also good at helping existing community members get to know and serve each other better.

CRAFTSMANSHIP

Exodus 35:31–35; 1 Chronicles 22:15–16 | The ability to design, build, maintain, or repair items or resources to facilitate the functioning of ministry or to help draw people to God. The creativity involved in this gift allows for ministry to take place on an intimate and personal level between individuals, or on a much grander scale by enabling creative ministry to entire congregations. Craftsmanship is often a worshipful gift using artistic expression that produces a spiritual response of strength and inspiration.

DISCERNMENT

Hebrews 5:14; 2 Colossians 2:8 | This is the divine ability to distinguish between truth and error, differentiating between good and evil, right and wrong. This gift requires a loving, wise, and humble heart that looks to the Holy Spirit for guidance. Discerners can help leadership or the individual stay the course, preventing others from being deceived. Their insights and wisdom are helpful when deciding how to handle complex situations or those situations that include gray areas.

DISCIPLESHIP

Matthew 28:18–20; Colossians 3:16 | Discipleship is the ability to bring health and maturity to the body of Christ through mentoring others in Christlikeness. Other gifts like encouragement, teaching, exhortation, wisdom, and leadership contribute to the fullness of applying this gift. The ultimate goal of Christian mentors is not to assert their authority over other believers but rather for their actions, words, and example to point those they disciple back to Christ's example and, ultimately, toward increased intimacy with and obedience of their heavenly Father.

DISTINGUISHING SPIRITS

Acts 6:16; 1 Corinthians 12:8–10 | Distinguishing spirits is a supernatural gift for the mature believer. Under the guidance of the Holy Spirit, it is a gift that takes aggressive opposition to the advancements of the evil one. Often used when harsh corrections or warnings need to be made. It is also often used with care in inner healing, or as an aid in deliverance (Ekballism).

EKBALLISM/DELIVERANCE

Matthew 10:1; Acts 5:16 | Ekballism is the ability to deliver people who are being harassed, attacked, oppressed, or possessed by a demonic presence. It is the special ability that God gives certain believers to bind and cast out evil spirits in the name of Jesus Christ.

ENCOURAGEMENT

Hebrews 10:24–25; 1 Thessalonians 5:11 | Encouragers are those moved by compassion for people and hope in the Lord. Generally, they are joyful, optimistic people who remind others of the faithfulness of God and readily identify his goodness, even in difficult situations. They also see God's favor and blessings within the character of individuals and are good at pointing out strengths in others in a genuine and meaningful way.

EVANGELISM

Ephesians 4:11; 2 Timothy 4:5 | Evangelism is a gift that enables others to more effectively share the gospel with unbelievers. Tenderheartedness and bravery manifest in the Christian who is obedient to regularly practice this gift. It is important for all Christians to share the gospel. For those Christians who have a special desire to participate in evangelism, it is important to look to Scripture and trust the guidance of the Holy Spirit when utilizing this gift.

EXHORTATION

1 Thessalonians 5:14; Romans 12:6–8 | A gift used to help strengthen those who are growing fainthearted or weak, faltering, or straying—being exhorted in such a way that they are motivated to live Christ-centered lives.

FAITH

1 Corinthians 12:8–10; Ephesians 2:8–9 | Faith is the special conviction God gives to some to be firmly persuaded of God's power and promises to accomplish his will and purpose. Those with the gift of faith display such a confidence in him and his Word that circumstances and obstacles do not shake that conviction. Those who possess this gift stir up others and increase the faith of the community.

GIVING

Romans 12:6–8; Proverbs 19:17 | This is the ability to discern God's guidance as to how he desires to provide resources for his kingdom and cheerfully contribute resources to God's work. Givers will often live ascetically so they have more to contribute to God's purposes.

HEALING

1 Corinthians 12:8–10, 28; Matthew 10:1 | The gift God gives to some to serve as a human instrument to cure illness and restore physical health. The healer is an intermediary through whom God's supernatural power is provided to meet a person's need for wholeness.

HELPING

1 Corinthians 12:28; Romans 12:10 | Helpers are the hardworking hands and feet of Christ. They are generally flexible and humble, not needing recognition or importance. They often work closely with leadership, finding creative ways to help share the burdens of ministry, and they are often down in the trenches attending to the fine details of daily endeavors, inside and outside the church.

HOSPITALITY

1 Peter 4:9–10; Hebrews 13:2 | Those with the gift of hospitality tend to be social and generous. They work well with community builders in creating a welcome atmosphere for community members, as well as creating a safe place for the lost to begin encountering the kingdom of God without necessarily having to enter a church building. Hospitable Christians are oftentimes used by God to provide for the needs of travelers, refugees, the poor, and the suffering by opening their homes for either long- or short-term ministry.

INNER-HEALING

Isaiah 61:1–3; Psalms 34:17–19 | This gift is given to believers who are charged to guide others, with God's lead and active participation, in healing brokenness of the soul and relieving emotional and mental distress.

INTERCESSION

Romans 8:26–27; Isaiah 62:6–7 | The special ability God gives to some to regularly pray for extended periods of time for matters that have been assigned to them by the Holy Spirit.

INTERPRETING DREAMS

Genesis 37:5–11; Acts 2:17; Revelations | This gift allows the believer to decipher messages from God communicated through their own visions or dreams or the visions and dreams of others. The Bible contains more than two hundred references or stories of significant, meaningful dreams.

KNOWLEDGE

1 Corinthians 12:8–10; 2 Chronicles 1:7–12 | Those who possess the gift of knowledge are perceptive, well informed, analytical, and studious. The gift of knowledge is used in the kingdom to research, remember, and make effective use of a variety of information on a number of diverse subjects, including those that may not seem particularly spiritual.

LEADERSHIP

Romans 12:6–8; Hebrews 13:7 | Leadership is a gift used to cast vision, motivate, and direct people to harmoniously accomplish the purposes of God. The leader sets goals in accordance to God's will and communicates these goals to others.

LOVE

John 15:1–17; 1 John 4:8 | God is our source of love! He has described it many times in his Word. We urge you to look at 1 Corinthians 13 concerning love and other spiritual gifts.

MARTYRDOM

Psalm 44:22; 1 Corinthians 13:1–3 | Throughout history, the body of Christ has undergone persecution to varying degrees. Many places in the world today are relatively safe for Christians, but there are still many locations where violence is a continuous threat to the Christian living or working there. Though no one should desire an atmosphere of violence, some have a higher tolerance for living and working in the midst of it. Martyrdom is the ability to cope well and possibly even be drawn to those situations where ultimate sacrifices of personal comfort, security, health, and life are likely to be required.

MERCY

Romans 12:6–8; Matthew 5:7 | This is the special gift whereby the Spirit enables believers to have exceptional compassion and empathy for those who are suffering. People with the gift of mercy often have a great capacity to demonstrate grace and love to even the most heinous of sinners; they inspire hope and forgiveness in the body of Christ. Those with the gift of mercy will speak words of compassion to help alleviate others in distress. They are concerned with caring for the broken with acts of love, restoring the soul.

MIRACLES

1 Corinthians 12:8–10, 28; Mark 16:17–18 | A special gift God gives some to act as a human intermediary, through whom he makes displays of supernatural power that are testament to his existence, his love, and his purpose on earth.

MISSIONARY

Acts 22:21; Mark 16:15 | Missionary is a gift manifesting a particularly strong desire to fulfill both the Great Commandment and Great Commission. This inventory focuses on foreign missions and the ability to bridge cultural gaps with spreading the gospel. We are all called to be missionaries—most of us to our own countries, cities, and communities. Occasionally, God sends some of his people to other cultures.

PASTORING

Ephesians 4:11; Acts 20:28 | A gift God gives to someone who will nurture a group of people, teaching by example with the goal of leading them to greater spiritual maturity and effective ministry. The role of a pastor is one that assumes long-term responsibility for leadership, spiritual care, protection, and guidance in a community.

PREACHING

Exodus 4:10–12; 1 Corinthians 2:1–5 | Preaching is a gift used to proclaim, explain, illustrate, and strongly urge the Word of God. Preachers encourage, challenge, and stir up other believers, making way for growth and spiritual maturity. Preachers are often gifted in rhetoric and do not mind addressing large crowds.

PROPHECY

Romans 12:6–8; Deuteronomy 18:18–22 | This gift enables the bearer to reveal truth to God's people for understanding or edification. Those with this gift are often fearless to deliver the truth of God with divine insight and authority so that people may have hope and direction and live for God. Prophets also play a big role in calling out identity and destiny in members of the body. They help appoint leaders with the church, through God's direction.

SERVICE

Romans 12:6–8; Mark 10:42–45 | To make a distinction with helping—a gift of support—service is the gift that requires the heart of a leader. People with this gift take initiative in their work with Christ to make a difference in tangible ways. Servers lead through their humility and sense of honor.

STORYTELLING

Acts 5:32; Psalms 107:2 | This gift has preserved the Word of God in the Christian oral traditions. It is used by those who memorialize the stories of God to further his kingdom in a variety of ways. If you have this gift, you may be particularly encouraged anytime you hear word of what God has done is someone's life. Soon thereafter, you may be eager to share these stories with others.

STEWARDSHIP

2 Corinthians 8; Luke 12:42–44 | All people are held accountable to steward the earth, and individuals are supposed to steward their own personal resources, like their time and talents. In addition to this, Christians are called specifically to steward the resources with which God blesses the church. Good stewards understand the value of what they are given and why it is entrusted to them. They see their possessions as God's, and they do not make decisions about how to use those resources apart from God.

TEACHING

Romans 12:6–8; Colossians 3:16 | Teaching is a gift given to enable the teacher to understand, clearly explain, and apply information so others may understand and learn. In this inventory, we focus on the gift of teaching as it pertains to the Word of God. This is not to say that God is not using this gift in you for his glory when it is applied to other circumstances or subjects of study.

TONGUES (INTERPRETING)

1 Corinthians 12:8–10; 1 Corinthians 14 | The special ability God gives to some to translate the message of one who speaks in tongues so that the community, in which the speaking of tongues occurs, will be edified.

TONGUES (SPEAKING)

1 Corinthians 12:8–10, 28; Acts 2:1–12 | The special ability God gives to some to speak prayer or praise in a language they have never learned. This gift is sometimes used to speak in a language not previously learned by the speaker so unbelievers can hear God's message in their own languages. Occasionally the tongues spoken are not necessarily known languages but spiritual ones; it is in these times that an interpreter is needed.

VOLUNTARY POVERTY

1 Corinthians 13:1–3; Acts 2:44–45 | A monastic gift of voluntary simplicity or poverty helps to identify with Jesus and the poor. It enables the bearer to be content with little for the purposes of God.

WISDOM

1 Corinthians 12:8–10; 1 Corinthians 2:6–13 | This gift is powered by an accurate, God-sourced worldview to make wise choices, give wise counsel, and teach wise truths. This gift enables us to discern the mind of God for his purposes.

WORSHIP

Psalms 150; 2 Chronicles 5:12–13 | This gift of worship is given to believers who are called to glorify God with creativity in a variety of forms. Often those who lead in this gift minister expressions of reverence and adoration that are edifying to others, compelling those around to follow in praise.

WRITING

1 John 2:12–14; Luke 1:1–4 | Those who possess this gift are often inspired by the Holy Spirit to formulate thoughts and ideas into meaningful written forms so that the reader will find courage, guidance, knowledge, or edification through the words shared with them.

> *Sometimes, when you have spent a long time rejecting the gifts of the Spirit and come to believe in them, you almost feel as if you are being born again. You feel as if you have a whole new Bible. By that latter statement I mean that the Gospels and Acts come alive for you in a way that they never have before. Things that you had relegated to the first century now become a possibility for today's church.*
> ~ *Jack Deere,* Surprised by the Power of the Spirit: Discovering How God Speaks and Heals Today

God gives us very specific gifts to enhance or empower the natural or learned skills he has designed us with. Sometimes, as with the widow asking the judge for bread, he gives us a gift purely because we keep asking for it. At other times, he knows we'll need, say, the gift of knowledge, because we've been faithful in hearing and obeying everything he's already told us. All the spiritual gifts are designed to empower us to minister God's heart to others.

FINISH THESE SENTENCES

I think the gifts of the Spirit are

I have benefited by having some of the gifts in the following ways:

I have benefited from the gifts on display in others in the following ways:

When I think about being faithful with the gifts I have and stewarding them well, I

I rate my ability to use the gifts I have as being _____ percent. I think I can grow that by

TRUTH

What is the truth about the value of the spiritual gifts you have? Mull over the following Scriptures and write down anything God shows you through them.

"Having gifts that differ according to the grace given to us, let us use them: if prophecy, in proportion to our faith; if service, in our serving; the one who teaches, in his teaching; the one who exhorts, in his exhortation; the one who contributes, in generosity; the one who leads, with zeal; the one who does acts of mercy, with cheerfulness." (Romans 12:6–8)

"The gifts and the calling of God are irrevocable (not able to be changed, reversed, or recovered; final)." (Romans 11:29 AMP)

"Since you are eager for manifestations of the Spirit, strive to excel in building up the church." (1 Corinthians 14:12)

"To equip the saints for the work of ministry, for building up the body of Christ." (Ephesians 4:12)

THINK IT THROUGH, FIGURE IT OUT

Examine each gift you know you have been given and ask yourself:
    Is it a gift for now or a gift for the future?

Does having the gift bring me closer to God and his people?

Are there other people within my sphere of influence who would appreciate me serving them with my gift? What opportunities do I have right now to use these gifts?

Have I given time and effort to develop the spiritual gifts I've been given?

Can I steward these gifts with faith to see them maximized in a way that will bless others?

Am I willing to wait for God to specifically direct my use of these gifts or am I ready to use them at any moment?

I've gone back to review the ways I've used gifts in the past and found …

ANGELA'S JOURNEY

From the age of four, I knew I wanted to be an actress. I loved entertaining my family with skits I had created. So when I graduated college, I went to the New York Film Academy to begin my acting career. On the plane ride there, I remember telling God I wasn't there to be a missionary; I was there to refine my craft. I loved the people I was meeting in the school. They had such different life experiences than mine, but somehow we shared a deep bond—the creativity that flowed through our veins. One day we did an exercise in class where we had to stand in front of everyone and say what we loved most passionately, and it couldn't be acting. I wanted to talk about painting in front of a room full of very cool kids from all over the world, but then God whispered *Really?* My hands began shaking, but I began to talk about how I passionately loved God. People began sharing their deeply personal struggles with me after that because they had seen my vulnerability and trusted me enough to share theirs.

I ended up having to move back home, live with my parents, and work as a waitress. I was devastated. Thankfully, I moved to Austin soon after to work with a talent manager. I was stretched in so many ways, and it was there that I truly grew as a person and an actress. My faith was tested constantly as I struggled to become a working actor. I invested so much time and money into classes, workshops, and headshots. I got a commercial here and there. I started to get roles in short films and do voiceovers. Then, finally, I landed some independent feature films. But I was far from where I wanted to be. The effort didn't add up to the results I had envisioned, but God was showing me progress and success by a different standard. He wanted me to see that it wasn't about which roles I had; it was about how I loved others—the impact I was having on my acting classmates' lives. God had shifted my heart to where I actually wanted to be a missionary to the film industry.

I had dreamed for years about moving to L.A., so when the time was right, I made the jump. I found a city so hungry for God, peace, and meaning, and I carried something that most don't have. I saw what all those years in Austin were preparing me for. When I was restless and just wanted to move forward as fast as I could, God was developing my character and my heart and teaching me how to minister to others. I just signed with an agent. I have some movies on Amazon. I'm still so far from where I envision myself being, but I have had countless opportunities to love people and to speak their identity to them in a city that can be so empty. My dreams of being a successful actress have not dimmed; they have only grown brighter when coupled with being a minister in Hollywood. I have submitted my dreams and my heart to God, and now I ask him to use me to love well. I am thankful for every day I get to stay in L.A. and pursue my dreams!

amharger.wixsite.com/angelahargeractress

Notes

Notes

WHY YOU DO IT

VALUES

I remember writing songs and having no idea what God would do with them. I would sit in our little prayer room for hours a day, screaming these songs at the top of my lungs because I believed that my voice mattered; and that if no one was listening, he was. He cared about my weak, little cry, my feeble, little yes. It was enough for him to take my broken mess and make it a melody. ... I am so grateful to have friends ... who dream beyond their means and allow God to do things in them and through them that so few people will ever see. Tonight I am going to bed so grateful for the people in my life, the things I get to be a part of, and the beauty of what God does with a little yes twenty years later.

~ Jake Hamilton, Facebook post

I've always placed a high value on learning, so much so that when my first child was already reading and writing her name at the age of four, I decided to keep teaching her at home rather than water down her learning opportunities in school. To this day she is passionate about reading and learning all she can about whatever interests her, and she puts her knowledge to work for business owners and into her own two businesses.

~ Sally K.

Our family values were about spending time together as a family and having fun. When we were raising our kids, we only had one computer, but games were usually played together. We watched films over again together with the boys saying the lines seconds before they were spoken. We valued reading and let the kids know it was okay to be in their own spaces doing "nothing." We always encouraged creativity in our little image bearers.

~ Val C.

My boss turns everything he touches into multi-million-dollar properties. He's a brilliant businessman. That's only part of it though. Very wealthy people rarely make the effort to thank the people who helped them get or stay that way, and they are usually completely out of touch with those of us who look on in awe and envy. His real talent is tied into his values of gratitude and humility, and they seem built in. I'll never forget how I felt when I saw that the license plate on his car read "GR8FUL."

~ Tiffany R.

And now we arrive at the regulators of all of this—your values—the principles you live by and the things you value in yourself and others. It's quite easy to put your life into sections when it comes to learning and choosing what will be important to you, what you will allow to shape your life. Keep in mind that I'm being overly generic here. We've all had unique upbringings and different kinds of people speaking into our lives.

> Childhood—what Mom and Dad say is how it is.
>
> Teen years—what Mom and Dad say can easily be rejected.
>
> College or young adult years—what Mom and Dad say doesn't count.
>
> Responsible adult years—Mom and Dad were actually wise sometimes.

I was raised in a two-parent household with five siblings. Dad was the breadwinner, and home life revolved around his schedule. We ate dinner together every night and then watched TV for a few hours before bed. We spent Sundays together—church, big dinner, and a family walk. We each had chores to complete. No cussing was allowed. Money was a tool, entrepreneurship was encouraged, reading and music appreciation were important.

The Irish culture is one in which you are always ready to help and support people, either with a ready ear or practical help—another value. I learned more values in boarding school, followed by different sets of values while staying with a family for a year in Spain, followed by three years living with other student nurses while earning my degree. It was those three years that changed my values the most, because that was when I became part of a church community that held total surrender and obedience to the Lord as the highest value of all. I was hooked.

To this day I value family time, entrepreneurship, reading, worship, knowledge, ministry, helping others, and radical obedience to the Lord. I'll invest my time and money here. I'll encourage it in others.

Rather than love, than money, than fame, give me truth.
~ Henry David Thoreau, Walden

Some of the more radical or religious denominations will open the door wide and then lock it with six deadbolts once you're inside. Then you're taught all the rules and taught how to tell others not in that church why they're wrong, how you're the godly elite who deserve a better place in heaven because you're following the rules so well, and how it's not healthy for you to be around family and old friends anymore so they don't sully your newfound holiness. If you're in a church like that, please run away and find a healthy community that doesn't twist Scripture into validation for its control.

Other churches will open the door so wide that you'll wonder if they have any values at all. The word *grace* is never matched with the words holiness and relationship, and you'll wonder why Jesus died at all if it doesn't seem to count for anything. But most churches have values that strengthen your walk with God rather than diminish it.

We can get into the mindset of only valuing what Jesus would value based, naturally, on what we've been told he values. Which is why Christians in the '70s started shutting down anything that had even touched something possibly ungodly. They all withdrew, and they became the world's largest bubble of people not wanting to be part of society—out of fear of being contaminated by the worldliness of their culture. But here's the thing: Jesus stepped into the world and stayed there. He didn't build a big house in the country and tell his chosen disciples to only hang out there because they'd be safe from polluted minds. He was in the world with them all the time. Not only that, he interacted with everyone and managed to keep his values intact.

And what were those values? Anything that made God look good, anything that celebrated his Father's gifts, and anything that brought people into a heart-to-heart connection with the Father was on the list.

God values every single personality type, skill, gift, and talent. God values agape love, community, giving, healing. God values counsel, wisdom, knowledge, understanding. God loves my list of values. I'm pretty sure he values yours too. The extra beauty of it all is that while we share some of the same values, our lists aren't identical. That means we get to bring everything God values to the world around us in our own unique ways. We've got the ammunition of heaven—the intimate knowledge and demonstration of God's heart—to pump into every aspect of society.

> *What we obtain too cheap, we esteem too lightly: it is dearness only that gives every thing its value. Heaven knows how to put a proper price upon its goods; and it would be strange indeed if so celestial an article as freedom should not be highly rated.*
> *~ Thomas Paine,* The American Crisis

ASSESSMENT

What are your top three most important values in life?

1.   2.   3.

Put a check mark beside the values you think are important below. Then fill in the amount of time you spend on each item you've marked per week.

VALUE	CHECK IF YES	TIME SPENT PER WEEK
FAMILY		
Logical thinking		
Time together		
Attending church		
Obedience		
Laughter		
Authenticity		
Eating together		
Creativity		
Teamwork		
FRIENDSHIPS		
Support		
Listening		
Acceptance		
Trust		
Mutual respect		
MONEY		
Hard work		
Promotions		
Job title		
Car, house, vacations		
Status		
Financial security		
Frugality		
Giving		
GROWTH		
Experience		
Self-development		
Learning/education		
The Arts		
Adventure		
Self-motivation		

VALUE	CHECK IF YES	TIME SPENT PER WEEK
HEALTH		
Rest		
Mental health		
Physical fitness		
Cleanliness		
GOD		
Ministry		
Connection with God		
Studying the Word		
Surrender		
HOLY LIVING		
Character		
Kindness		
Helping others		
Perseverance		
Honesty/integrity		
LOYALTY		
Hope		
Faith		
Humility		
Excellence		

Here's the kicker. The things you have spent the most time on are the things you really care about—your real values. Everything else is just words. Because if you give time and attention to something, it's important. If you don't, it's not. Are you happy with the results?

We choose our values because we believe that shaping our lives by them will give us the results we want. So if, for example, we believe that bending the truth a little is okay, that means we are okay with presenting a distorted view of reality to those around us.

> *Nothing in this world can take the place of persistence. Talent will not; nothing is more common than unsuccessful men with talent. Genius will not; unrewarded genius is almost a proverb. Education will not; the world is full of educated derelicts. Persistence and determination alone are omnipotent.* ~ Calvin Coolidge

FINISH THESE SENTENCES

I'd like to/would rather not change up my days to focus exclusively on my values because

I think Jesus sees my values as

I think the Holy Spirit will/will not support my values because

I'm going to give more time to live by my values by

My motive for living according to my values is

TRUTH

What is the truth about how important your values are? Mull over the following Scriptures and write down anything God shows you through them.

"But be doers of the word, and not hearers only, deceiving yourselves ... the one who looks into the perfect law, the law of liberty, and perseveres, being no hearer who forgets but a doer who acts, he will be blessed in his doing." (James 1:22,25)

"As you wish that others would do to you, do so to them." (Luke 6:31)

"Pray for us, for we are sure that we have a clear conscience, desiring to act honorably in all things." (Hebrews 13:18)

"Those who act faithfully are his delight." (Proverbs 12:22).

"Everyone serves the good wine first, and when people have drunk freely, then the poor wine. But you have kept the good wine until now." (John 2:10)

THINK IT THROUGH, FIGURE IT OUT

Looking back at your values chart, list the five top things you have spent the most time on this week. If it was an off week compared to your usual time invested in these values, change up your list to reflect that.

1.
2.
3.
4.
5.

Fill out the chart below based on the percentage of time you gave to each section of values in the earlier assessment in this chapter.

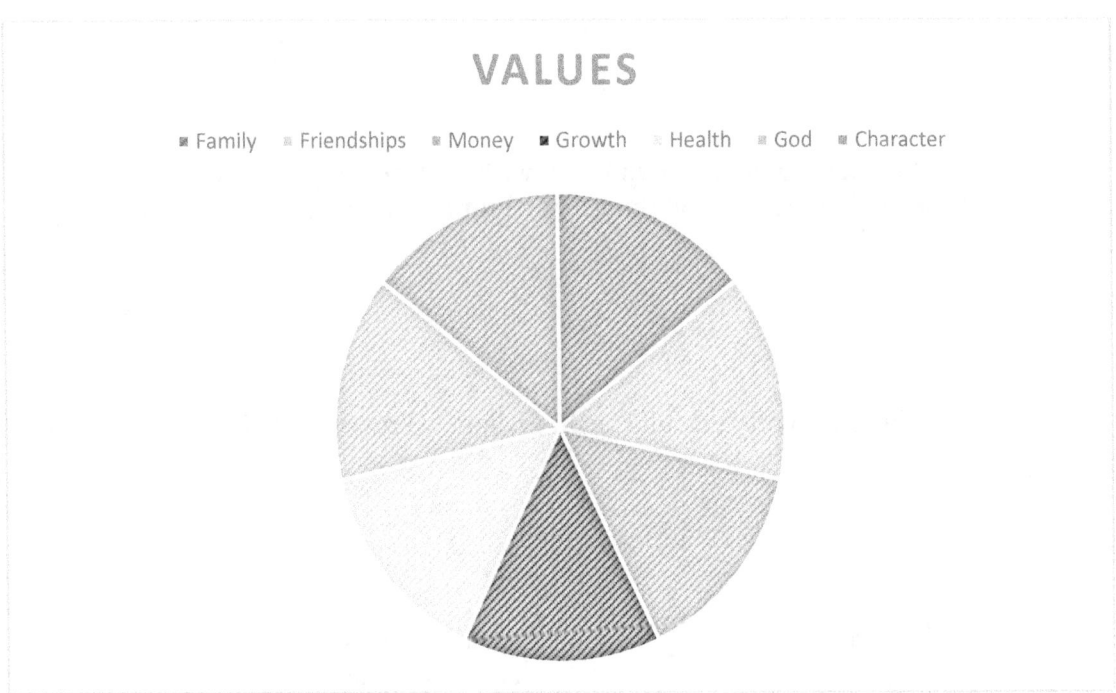

List the top three areas you thought were values but your time log reflects they really aren't.

1.
2.
3.

How does looking at your actual top values and/or lack of value make you feel?

Is there anything you're determined to change? Why?

> *I don't think that God says, "Go to church and pray all day and everything will be fine." No. For me God says, "Go out and make the changes that need to be made, and I'll be there to help you."* ~ Elvia Alvarado, Don't Be Afraid, Gringo

PERRY MARSHALL'S JOURNEY (LATE FORTIES)

I grew up in a very much lower middle-class family. My dad worked for a nonprofit organization for a few years, and later he switched to being a pastor at a church. In that move we went to middle class instead of lower middle class. My parents were super conservative and very devout Christians. We went to a Christian school through sixth grade and were very, very indoctrinated with its excessively conservative curriculum. The virtue of it was we knew what the rules were and we knew there was no real question about all that, and I got a very good grounding in theology and Bible stories. And on top of that, we went to this super expositional, hardcore Bible-teaching church where they would talk about the Greek and the Hebrew meanings of everything, which developed my intellectual capacities and my ability to read literature.

Nobody around me had any real technical inclination, but my curiosity about electronics, electricity, and science was insatiable. I started playing with motors, lightbulbs, and batteries and then moved onto radios, stereo systems, and all of that. The only way to do all the experiments I wanted to do was to turn it into a business, so I designed speakers and built them, and I also did a little bit of electronics. By the time I was a senior in high school, I was selling my speakers at a local stereo dealer alongside other known brands.

In my junior year, my parents went out of town for my dad's cancer treatments, and I spent about a month living in the home of a family that we knew from church. The father, a Korean immigrant to the US, was a professor at the University of Nebraska and also a highly paid management consultant. I had some very pivotal conversations with him. My dad was raised by a tobacco farmer. There weren't any luxuries, and there wasn't any extra to go along; it was just the hard life of a farm family. That was my dad's conception of work, yet here was Dr Lee and his family living a life of luxury. I gained a different idea of what work actually was, what it meant, and what it could do. I quit my janitorial job and started my speaker business in earnest.

What was forming was a young man with a great deal of respect for traditional paths to success—like a university, climbing the ladder, and paying your dues—but who also had this entrepreneurial, technical streak where I just wanted to pursue things. I decided to study electrical engineering. My high school guidance counselor saw the way I was handling the loss of my dad, and she could tell that I had a very good faith community behind me. She saw how I was growing amid all this and predicted I would be the most successful person to come out of the class I was in. I managed to get into the honors program. Dr Knoll, my favorite professor of all time, was fascinated that I could understand both people and things and said I could do very well in technical sales and eventually be the president of the company.

Most of my twenties was just a big, long struggle. I got out of school, worked as an engineer for two or three years, got laid off from the engineering job, went into a bitter struggle of a sales job for two years, and ended up getting fired. By the age of twenty-nine, I felt a lot of shame for my lack of progress. It was just a steady diet of failure. I was five years out of college and nothing I had done had been particularly successful. Entrepreneurs are misfits. People who challenge things, ask questions, and are extremely curious end up being troublemakers; and they're difficult for employers to deal with. I ended up getting into a multi-level marketing (MLM) business, which was a total bust, but it taught me a lot of stuff about people and about how to tell stories, which was a very important part of my future. It also gave me a deep appreciation for the level of desperation budding entrepreneurs have to do what they want to do to be free, have their own businesses, and be successful.

The first time my talents were really recognized and valued professionally was when I switched to another job successfully selling industrial hardware and software. It was almost like therapy. I eventually got stock options in the company. Four years later I started my own business doing seminars, selling information, and teaching entrepreneurs. About the same time that I started my business, I switched from being in the evangelical corner of the world to being in the Holy Spirit, charismatic corner of the world. It took a couple of years, but I started to figure out there was some very deep stuff going on, and I witnessed some miracles in person. It all switched me into a completely different way of expressing Christianity.

I can now be myself to a significant degree around a substantial number of people, but I'm not there yet. My wife and I went through a perfect storm of hardships when we took on some new challenges with business, marriage, and two adoptions. We had all those challenges stacked on top of each other to where I ended up with my back against the wall, with nowhere to go other than to just go deeper into my relationship with God. I spend every first hour of every day praying, meditating, and doing God time, and it's the most valuable thing that I do all day. That's been one of the biggest shifts in my life.

I think, in a large sense, I have figured out what I'm on earth for. I'm here to heal the rift between science and religion and provoke a second renaissance. That means bridging a lot of chasms. I think I'm really just at the foothills of accomplishing what needs to be accomplished and what is possible to accomplish. I think I have a much bigger impact to make on the world than I've made so far. Everything so far has been a prelude.

www.perrymarshall.com

NOTES

Notes

PASSION 8

I am selectively passionate about things, but the phrase "still waters run deep" comes to mind in describing how that might look to someone else: you might not realize how important something is to me if you're looking for a loud or active emotional response. My very introverted, thinking self will take the realization that I feel strongly about something and prompt me to ask why I feel that way. I will analyze it and realize that the passion-inspiring thing aligns with a value I hold, or undergirds a gift I may possess, and it will likely be something I feel strongly about (and endeavor to act upon) for the rest of my life.

~ Peggy R.

Sometimes I lead by principle and not passion because I do not take the time to discover the passion, understand the why of the passion, own the passion, or let the passion fuel my imagination.

~ Lance B.

Passion is the voice in my head/spirit that tells me, c'mon Eric, let's go (or move your a__!) when I'm out for a run and then have to push up a hill, or about to have to lift some weights I don't really want to lift (basically every time I do squats). I went out for a run for the first time with my Daniel (fourteen), and when we got to a hill and it got hard, he yelled out loud at himself, "C'mon, Daniel!" to will himself to keep going up the hill ... kind of a proud, yet scary, moment for me. Genetics are awesome.

~ Eric T.

Passion pushes me through fear. It shoves aside the doubts even as doubt shoves back, yet passion is stronger because passion is filled with love and hope and the feeling that through whatever I am doing in this passion, whatever it is meant for me to accomplish, it will make a marked difference to someone besides myself. It will bring that someone hope, or love, or joy in a dark place, or nudge them onto a better path. My passion is not meant for me alone, but more importantly, it is meant to spread outward for good.

~ Lynn G.

Passion is usually thought of as a fiery emotion, one that's displayed loudly and seems out of control. Maybe that's true for the extroverts, but not so much for the introverts. We often call the death of Jesus the passion of Christ. There was no frenzy in his sacrifice, although the Pharisees' desire to see him murdered could be called uncontrollable. So passion is more of a strong or intense emotion that can be displayed in either loud or quiet ways. Jesus was passionate about our becoming one with the Father, and his passion led him to give up his life to make that happen.

Passion keeps the bellows moving on the fire inside.

I think God added passion to our blueprints in the same moment he breathed life into us. It's like the gas for the car—you're not going anywhere important without the fuel to power the engine.

Passion is that feeling of being fully alive when you are looking at, learning about, or doing something. I might feel fully alive when I'm writing, whereas you might feel that way when you're standing on top of a mountain in Croatia with your best friends. It matters. You might not be able to fully explain why it matters, but I'll tell you why: it's because you're wired to come alive when you can taste pieces of your destiny.

What you usually find with passion, when you look at it logically, is that it lines up with your design—your personality type, your natural gifts and talents, your spiritual gifts, and your values. This thrills me, because yet again, it proves that God cares about all the details of your makeup. Not only did he design you to be a unique facet of humanity who fills spaces no one else can, he also gave you passion to fuel the journey and enrich your enjoyment of it all.

> David was extremely passionate about protecting God's reputation and honor (Psalm 69:9; 119:139).
>
> God was passionate about saving a remnant of his people and replanting them (2 Kings 19:30–31).
>
> God was, and is, passionate about establishing relationship with us (Isaiah 9:6–7).
>
> Those who met Jesus were passionate in telling everyone they met about him (Mark 7:35–37).
>
> Jeremiah's passion to speak God's truth made him incapable of doing otherwise (Jeremiah 20:9).

Some passions are worth dying for. The disciples were willing to die if it meant more people could have the one-in-one relationship with the Father Jesus died for. Parents will die for their children to go on living. Soldiers will die for their countries to be safe from invaders. Missionaries will die for the truth to be heard. When the purpose is to bring life and life abundantly, passion is wonderful. "It is always good to be made much of for a good purpose, and not only when I am present with you, my little children, for whom I am again in the anguish of childbirth until Christ is formed in you!" (Galatians 4:18–19).

But life isn't only about passion for Jesus, it's about being passionate for every single gift he has given us. We need to live celebrating it all. We need to utilize and grow and live it all out in a way that blesses many. You're not just a parent or a church member or someone's kid. You're a perfect mix of experience and personality and talent and knowledge and passion that matters.

YOU matter. Your life matters.

YOUR being here matters.

AND your being here being you matters most of all.

You knowing that is something I'm passionate about. Never be embarrassed about your passion for developing your gifts and interests, because even if you can't see a good purpose in any of them now, God could be fueling your passion for something specifically because it's really important for you to use at a later date.

Not everyone is going to be enthused about your passion(s). We're all wired differently, so your passion might even look laughable to some judgmental people who haven't even tried to understand what's going on in your heart. Then there are those people who seem to make it their passion to squish the life and joy out of anything you get excited about. Trust me, only the devil gets satisfaction out of that, so they're doing his work for him. Keep going. Keep learning, taking classes, asking questions, practicing, reading, listening, watching. It'll all make sense some day.

We must listen to and value each other's life message, because nobody can say it all. Never belittle someone else's godly passion.
~ Rick Warren, founder and senior pastor of Saddleback Church

FINISH THESE SENTENCES

For me, passion means

When I think of how my passion lines up with God's design of me, I think

The last time I felt fully alive was when I was

I think other people think my passion is

I think God thinks their judgment and/or encouragement of my passion is

I think my passion will help me

TRUTH

What is the truth about appreciating your passion? Mull over the following Scriptures and write down anything God shows you through them.

"Do not be slothful in zeal." (Romans 12:11)

"Who gave himself for us to ... purify for himself a people for his own possession who are zealous for good works." (Proverbs 24:32)

"Since we have such a hope, we are very bold." (2 Corinthians 3:12)

"Jesus said to them, 'My food is to do the will of him who sent me and to accomplish his work.'" (John 4:34)

"So we do not lose heart. Though our outer self is wasting away, our inner self is being renewed day by day." (James 1:2–4)

THINK IT THROUGH, FIGURE IT OUT

What are you truly passionate about? Part of the answer can be found in the results of your values chart, but that is usually more about how you spend your time, and how you align with your values, than the things that make you feel truly alive.

Looking at your bookshelves, what genres are most of your books in? For example, mine are mostly self-help, counseling, and women's fiction books.

What magazines do you, or have you ever, subscribed to?

What groups have you enjoyed being part of over the course of your life?

What hobbies or interests have you had over the course of your life?

What five topics do you know a lot about?
1.   2.   3.
4.   5.

What five products do you know a lot about?
1.   2.   3.
4.   5.

Out of all your answers above, which interests would you call passions?

As I've mentioned before, you are a unique collection of many parts, and when you start to look at everything you have done so far in this workbook and put it all together, you get to see where you fit. You see where your niche is in life—for now, because as we know, life changes. Fill out the chart below with the top answers from the previous chapters and this one. Some may overlap, so add those twice. (I've adapted these questions from a course by Perry Marshall, a Christian genius who helps businesses customize their marketing and business models to make the businesses as successful as possible—perrymarshall.com. His story is at the end of the previous chapter.)

GIFTS	PASSIONS	VALUES	SKILLS

Does anything strike you as interesting? Write about it below.

Secondly, contact at least six people who have known you for at least three years and ask them this:

I'm taking a course and can only complete one of the assignments with your help. All I need is your answer to this question: What do you see as my unique gifts, passions, values, and skills? What do I naturally do well? I need a reply by _____ [2-4 days from now].

Alternatively, post the request on social media. People seem to be more interactive there. Try to pull people from different parts of your life—friends, church, work, clubs, neighbors, relatives, etc., so as to get as accurate a result as possible. We act differently around different people at times, and this way, all of your abilities will be highlighted.

Fill their answers into the table below.

GIFTS	PASSIONS	VALUES	SKILLS

These are your strengths. These are the areas where your gifts, skills, passion, and values fit. You can summarize your niche in life into one to three sentences, along the lines of: I accomplish _____ by doing _____. For example:

> I solve hard problems by deconstructing complex systems into their component parts.
>
> I gently and methodically persuade by writing short punchy stories.
>
> When something needs to be done, I get through to the right person and get 'er done.

Write yours below.

Knowing where you can contribute maximum value is crucial to knowing where to give most of your time, and your daily life won't be wasted anymore.

ANNICE'S JOURNEY (LATE THIRTIES)

Growing up, I valued my ability to get lost in my imagination. I was able to retreat to a place of perfection during childhood beatings, and in that place I clung to the hope of one day being free from the reality of the ugliness around me. Time would move so slow outside me, but inside time served me. Time was magical. It was my own fairytale.

I am a P.K. (preacher's kid). I got saved at the age of seven, and almost every day I would cry out for God to save me from the grips of hell I was going through, not realizing I had become my own intercessor for my future self. As time passed, I grew restless with the pain because I had no vision of purpose for the pain itself. I had so many questions as a child. Why was I born into a family with all this noise? Why is my mother like this? Why can't I wake from what seems like everlasting torment? But I was able to escape—in my imagination, life did not show up like this.

I became a runner. I ran as fast as I could and as hard I could straight into the arms of stupid. Funny how pain has a way of causing one to lose all intellect and wisdom—you live in a place of carpe diem or eat, drink, and be merry today, right now, and forget tomorrow. I knew better. I know 80 percent of what happened to me was because of my own inability to access truth in wisdom. Having a baby at seventeen, being homeless at eighteen, selling drugs, managing clubs ... I was always trying to run away from a past by running and crashing into my future. But God remembered the prayers of a seven-year-old girl. He caused her prayers to be remembered in time, and he answered. He came and rescued my future. He stopped time by holding my times and seasons in his hands. We had a hard road. He never gave up, even though I did a few times. Tragedy struck a few times. I walked away from wisdom on occasion, but He stood in wisdom. His faithfulness changed me.

In the beauty of this moment, you are reading this and at the same time, we are both on a journey to a better future. In time we shall see how the matter will fall. I suspect, call it a prophetic hunch, we will look back at this moment in time, and we shall agree that in the end it has all been well worth it. I have not attained the goal yet, but I forget those things which are behind and praise him going forward.

I believe in being a living legacy, so I am distributing the wealth of glory now. As I get it, I give it. I want to see people live in God in the now, and I'm determined to help them do it through preaching, teaching, loving, writing, and just being transparent. I hope I am accomplishing this for him and for them. The beauty of my journey is I am still coming through it.

annicesilimon.com

Notes

Notes

DREAMS 9

Something I've secretly always wanted to do but never thought I quite have what it takes: to be at least a semi-recognized, semi-famous composer. On a more realistic note: to just get my music out there, published, and performed.
~ Walter P.

I dream that a kid in Tanzania becomes a Nobel prize-winning scientist and I'm lucky enough to recognize that kid and remember the day when we brought books to the school that helped make that possible. I have this kid's picture on my computer. He loves science. It could happen.
~ Lisa M.

I dream of selling millions of books. Some of them get made into movies. I get to say no to people who want to do dumb TV stuff with them. I also dream the whole world hears that it's awesome and loved. I give away cooler stuff than Oprah. Here. Have a castle.
~ Miles O.

I've had a strong affinity toward all animals, but particularly dogs, since I was a young child. As my life progressed, I found that my love of dogs and people, and helping them have good relationships together, was very fulfilling. I've been doing it for over thirty years, and I don't get tired of seeing the magic when two species connect positively.
~ Diana S.

I would love to go on an archaeological dig at some point in my life.
~ Cathy B.

I dream of writing characters that are loved long after I'm gone, and of sharing biblical values and truth in a way that touches hearts and changes lives through writing and teaching. I want to see both my children loving and living for God with all they have and all they are. I want to continue to enjoy my marriage, until the day I meet Jesus and realize the biggest dream of all: hearing him say, "Well done, good and faithful servant."
~ Debbie O.

Throughout life we often get stuck in a rut. We wonder why we bother to do the daily eat, sleep, work routine that never ends. It feels so bad because we can't see or feel any life in what we're doing. We fail to feel fully alive in the moments of each day. Some would say that's because our attitudes suck, or because we're not praying enough, or blah de blah blah. They have no idea what they're talking about (unless your attitude stinks for real). We're created for life, for living in the moment, and for planning ahead with full living in mind.

> *The dreamers of the day are dangerous men, for they may act on their dreams with open eyes, to make them possible. ~ T.E. Lawrence*

Dreams change that. They change us because they give us hope that's powerful enough to get us out of our ruts and fill us with the energy to reach forward into the *more*. We can hope for a maximized life and rich relationships. We can dream of having enough money to do less work and spend our leisure time on more enjoyable things. We can dream of living so well that our lives are gifts to others.

People say to do what you love and the money will follow. That's hogwash. I love eating, but it's not going to cause boxes of money to show up at my door if I quit my day job to stuff my face more.

So what are your dreams? What have you pictured yourself doing since you were a child? Where would I find you if I paid off all your debts and gave you $5,000 and two weeks off? Where's the point of convergence—where your personality, talents, skills, spiritual gifts, values, and passions merge and you become the power force you always were? Some dreams I've heard from people are:

    I want to write best-selling books.

    I dream of being a well-known speaker.

    I want to be a famous artist.

    I want to be a famous actor.

So many dreams of wanting to be seen and heard. The dream of getting public attention can be part of God's plan for us. He wants us to know his love and share his love, and it's easier to do that on a large scale with an audience. Others have dreams like:

    I dream of running a billion-dollar company.

    I want to build hundreds of subdivisions.

    I dream of giving away other people's money.

    I want to discover the cure for Alzheimer's.

Love makes dreams like those richer. When you do things out of love for the people you want to minister to, cure, build beautiful homes for, sell your art to, share your wisdom and insight with—you get to enrich their lives with all you are.

> *The actual number of famous people in 2013, according to* Wired Magazine, *was 0.00041, or 1 in every 10,000. That means your chances of ever being a household name are slim to none. What if you're meant to write or draw or act or speak and you're never famous? You keep doing what you're made for.*

Imagine you've worked incredibly hard to get to where you are.

You've written more than ten books.

You've taken every class on speaking you could find, and you've taught for free wherever they'd have you.

You've spent decades working on your artistic skills.

You've served in every position you could find that would teach you more about how to start and lead a company well.

You've spent decades improving your acting skills, and you've kept working every job imaginable to fund the dream.

You've done all that and you're still not a household name. Are you okay with being one of the 9,999 in every 10,000 people who will never be famous? Are you okay with being you, with your heavenly mix of everything God gave you? Are you okay with giving that to the world as a gift? Because you *are* God's gift to the world. Not some day. *Today. Tomorrow.* Yesterday you were too. God gave you life and filled you with gifts that made you feel that life. He's given you the ability to bring heaven to earth. He told you to do everything you can to connect people with his heart and make them whole. Do you need to be famous to do that? Your life purpose is to be lived out every day in every moment. It's all the little things. It's all those interactions with people. It's all your skill going into doing each thing well. No matter where you are or how many big bodacious dreams you have, know that simply because you have it in your heart to love people, your heart will be in the right place to maximize their blessings if and when those dreams materialize. And that's the best place for your heart to be.

> *If you have a vision of prosperity that doesn't also benefit other people, then your vision is too small.* ~ Bill Johnson

FINISH THESE SENTENCES

I want/don't want to be famous because

I am enough right now because

I minister love by

I think my heart is ready for my dreams to come true because

I will hold onto my dreams because

I would like to invest in my dreams by

Jesus thinks my dreams are

DREAMS

TRUTH

What is the truth about your dreams? Mull over the following Scriptures and write down anything God shows you through them.

"I am sure of this, that he who began a good work in you will bring it to completion at the day of Jesus Christ." (Philippians 1:6)

"Many are the plans in the mind of a man, but it is the purpose of the Lord that will stand." (Proverbs 19:21–21)

"Bless the Lord O my soul, and all that is within me, bless his holy name! Bless the Lord, O my soul, and forget not all his benefits, ... who crowns you with steadfast love and mercy, who satisfies you with good so that your youth is renewed like the eagle's." (Psalm 103:1–5)

"Hope that is seen is not hope. For who hopes for what he sees? But if we hope for what we do not see, we wait for it with patience." (Romans 8:24–25)

"[He] died for us so that whether we are awake or asleep we might live with him. Therefore encourage one another and build one another up, just as you are doing." (1 Thessalonians 5:1–11)

BILL'S JOURNEY (EARLY SEVENTIES)

I was always a very distracted dreamer and visionary in my Catholic elementary school. While these very traits were my markers of excellence later in life, they were apparently the worst things about me in school, but I got through because of my ability to talk. I took an aptitude test when I was ten, and the results said something to the effect of my being able to sell a hog farm to a rabbi.

My father was awful to me all the time—he'd constantly criticize me, beat me, shout at me. I was never good enough, so there was no point in ever trying to be. But he was stunning with people, the best manager. He knew everyone's name. He became vice president and then president of that company. He was a very religious Catholic, and he beat into me the knowledge that you reap what you sow. He apologized later and cried a lot over it, and we became very good friends. He told me, "I wish I was able to say you are so imaginative and so bright and always the leader. I wish I'd encouraged that. You needed my approval so you played football. I would have approved of you even without the football."

I suffered my way through being an altar boy. The priest drank a lot, and I thought all the rules were stupid. I hated church, and I was sexually abused by a priest when I was about ten, which took me away from God for thirty years. Catholic school was very good at discouraging me from doing anything.

I also had a learning disability—dyslexia. The teachers called me dumb, but my mother fed my curiosity by putting books in front of me that were interesting, so much so that by the age of seven, I knew I wanted to be psychologist. As the only boy at home with four sisters who all had their times of the month at the same time, my need for understanding made sense.

In high school I was part of a big mixed group as one of the leaders. We were all very bright. We did some dumb stuff—nothing bad. Some of us offered to run the local gas station. We put that station on the map and made money. Between that and football and being into hot rods, school was not a high priority, but I managed to get a football scholarship to college.

I loved every minute of my college psychology classes, especially when studying the brain. I married a journalism student, Sandra. She talked me into going to Uganda with the peace corps, teaching at a boarding school and college campus of 800 boys and men 6,000 feet up in the mountains. Some underhanded things had been going on, and I ended up taking on the role of headmaster—something I hadn't a clue about. I was twenty-five years old and felt completely helpless. That job provided me with a lot of understanding of the community, especially because we had students from eight different tribes. I got them to talk about tribal conflict and come up with their own solutions as to how to resolve it, bringing a lot of unity that country hadn't experienced before. The minister of education then asked me to help him build a nationwide program from scratch.

Idi Amin started causing trouble. Months later, three English guys and I went for a drink in town and were arrested for having outlawed beards. We were left to melt on a mud floor for days and then forced to watch the execution of some African soldiers and our jailer. We were let go, but I had nightmares for years after that. A few months later we had two hours' notice to leave the country. Three times a soldier put a machine gun through the window and pointed it at us on our way to Kampala. We were one trigger pull away from death. We made it out of the country, despite meeting death many times. I should not be here. I wasn't a believer, but God was watching over us. I would go right back in a minute.

We moved to work in the peace corps office in Washington. Two professors who had written a book about my work in Uganda invited me to Ohio to do grad school, and so I became a gradual student. I worked for the dean of psychology and the dean of business and got my PhD in organizational change in psychology. I helped the provost create the first program for organizational psychology in the state.

We took off to travel in Spain and started thinking of living there and never going back when Exxon offered me the job of director for organizational development. I stayed in that job for ten years and traveled all over the world. I started my own consulting company in 1985. Sandra and I had no kids, and we got divorced after being married for twenty years. We should have just stayed friends from the beginning. I was doing great work and enjoying it, but it took its toll on my heart—in 2005 I had a heart attack. I died three times in the ambulance, and they filled me with enough nitroglycerin to blow up a block. The ICU nurse asked me "Do you believe in God?" "I kinda do," I said. "Well, we have no bloody idea why you're still alive, so God obviously doesn't want to take you yet."

I met Elaine, my wife, online in 2006. We first met at a local restaurant and six hours later we were still talking, but she didn't want to move forward unless I knew Jesus. When I started going to the Vineyard church with Elaine, I began to realize Jesus had been with me my whole life. We married a year later.

I'd coached a lot of men and led men's groups all my life and knew it was part of my calling. You really find your joy helping other people. I started the church's men's ministry, and it's been a wonderful experience. I teach them about communicating their relational needs and act as somewhat of a senior coach to the church leadership team. I also work at a Christian counseling center. When I'm gone, I want people to be able to say that I gave them the practical tools to be relational, that others can say they see Jesus in them, and that I helped them become more like Jesus.

www.allamericanspeakers.com/speakers/5079/Bill-Brendler

NOTES

DREAMS

Notes

WHEN PURPOSE BEGINS

The Journey 10

When I was younger, I didn't have many friends. I felt like I'd always be alone. All I had was God and my family, but by college I was able to start over and just be myself again. Before that I just walled myself off after allowing others to hurt and bully me. I hid away in music and books. It still took until I was in my mid-twenties before I really knew who I was. I was finally ready for God to bring my husband into my life when I was twenty-nine. Looking back, I realize that if I'd met him sooner, I wouldn't have been ready for a relationship anyway. That time of focusing on God, school, music, and books led to what I would eventually do with my life: take care of our kids, write, and eventually get back to using my degree. He brought me back to teaching music and playing again. The journey may not make sense with all the detours along the way, but if we trust God, he will bring us to where we were meant to be.

~ Shari A.

Seasons are fluid, much as seasons are in the natural world. And we may camp in one stage for a very long time; stalemated, it would seem; developing fruit that takes longer to ripen yet ripening all the same. I didn't determine my very own relationship with God until I was in my fifties, the "stripped down" season—sans husband, sans church, sans children—in a season of abandonment and aloneness. Maybe it is possible to have the seasons occur in a different order for different people, or maybe it is just part of the fluidity of life to drift back and forth in a way peculiar to each person. I find my own journey seems to be taking a path through several seasons simultaneously.

~ Ann G.

The wholeness I've arrived at later in life was affected by either reaching or not reaching my dreams and goals, especially those linked to my passions. Embracing relationships that honored and encouraged me in achieving those dreams was critical in that. Over my life, I've realized I need to hang in there during the downs and embrace the ups. One usually follows the other, and a few really close friends help traverse this crazy thing we call life a lot better than many acquaintances. This means I don't strive to make everyone I meet a close friend.

~ Sharon B.

We each have our own journey to travel, and while many may say that journey is planned by God, it's ours to choose because we have free will. That said, God knows us. He knows our design, personality mix, skills, talents, spiritual gifts, and perspectives on life. He is able to judge quite easily what we'll pick and how often we'll go around the mountain—to learn that one lesson that's crucial for handling the next stage with aplomb. He knows when people will cheer us on, when we'll feel abandoned, when we'll ride the waves of success, when we'll wonder if we'll ever survive the emotional trauma of loss.

"If I make my bed in Sheol, you are there!" (Psalm 139:8). God knows he's enough in any stage, but much of our journeys is about finding that to be true. We grow up in faith, hope, and love. And at the end of our days, we find that the greatest of these is, indeed, love—his love in us and toward us, his love through us.

One thing I am adamant about is that everything *doesn't* happen for a reason. That would imply that God is Machiavellian (using clever lies and tricks in order to get or achieve something). He is far from that, but he wastes nothing. He can find gold in anything you have been through and turn it into something beautiful. It's not that he recycles. He takes what was born, what was created in you through those times, and uses all those individual creations as the chief ingredients for something spectacular.

> *It may be hard for an egg to turn into a bird: it would be a jolly sight harder for it to learn to fly while remaining an egg. We are like eggs at present. And you cannot go on indefinitely being just an ordinary, decent egg. We must be hatched or go bad.* ~ C.S. Lewis

We meet people along the way who encourage us, or love us unconditionally, or put us down, or make life difficult. How we respond to their words and actions can change everything. I know I keep repeating myself in saying that we can't put our lives into boxes, but having a framework can help us to understand what stage of life we are in and how valuable it is.

You might think that by now, having been through so much on your life journey already, you'd be perfect; but when Jesus said we should be perfect just like God is, the better translation is "complete." We have all of heaven open for use and ready for the taking. We can be complete and lacking in nothing. The only thing holding us back from being as complete as God is our openness to going after and receiving what he has on offer as we travel. The word also means mature ... but let's not get ahead of ourselves.

I've put together an outline of what a "normal" life journey might look like, inspired tremendously by Tony Stolzfus's book *The Calling Journey: Mapping the Stages of a Leader's Life Call—A Coaching Guide* with a view to helping you understand your own journey and what God might be doing in and through you during each stage.

NURTURED (HOME)

You've figured out which subjects you enjoy in school.

Your talent is encouraged and occasionally celebrated by parents and teachers, or you feel invisible.

You've figured out how to follow the rules and fit into a schedule set in place by others, or your favorite words are *no* and *why*.

You think you know a lot more than you do about life.

You're willing to take risks, try everything, experience it all, or you're scared of trying anything.

You don't like anyone telling you what to do or prefer that they do.

PARTIALLY SUPPORTED (POST HIGH SCHOOL)

No one is there to rush in and fix your mistakes, or your parents still try and fix everything.

You experience failure.

You know what kinds of people you enjoy or dislike being around.

You choose your own values.

Life isn't what you expected.

You question everything you learned growing up.

You determine your own relationship with God.

You value your parents' input more.

INDEPENDENT

You gain valuable work experience.

You learn how to be fully responsible for your choices.

You gain better communication skills.

You learn how to lead or follow.

You are more willing to work through your weaknesses.

You don't feel as if you are living according to your purpose.

You reflect on and reevaluate earlier life experiences.

You possibly experience the worst emotional times of your life and your faith deepens, or you abandon God for a while.

SETTLED

You are humbler about admitting your weaknesses and getting help.

You feel more complete as a person than you ever have.

You understand yourself.

You go after your interests and don't let fear stop you.

RECOGNIZED AND STRIPPED DOWN

Your skills and talents are recognized and valued.

You're given opportunities to shine.

This could be the time of your biggest failure or letdown.

This could be the time of your greatest success.

You surrender to God completely.

WHOLENESS

_A_ You've figured out what you're on this earth for.

You're secure in who you are and what you give to others.

You care more about helping others before helping yourself.

Your mask is gone.

or

_B_ You spend your time regretting past mistakes.

You resent how you were treated.

You neglect or perhaps mistreat even those who care for you.

LEGACY (SOME NEVER REACH THIS LEVEL, SEE WHOLENESS B)

You are your best self, completely comfortable in your own skin.

You don't need to impress anyone.

You're a light on a hill.

You serve others well with your lifetime of walking with God, knowledge, people skills, and experience.

You're happy to have lived a fulfilling life and are paving the way for others to live well.

I was nurtured well growing up, and my life followed the pattern I've mentioned up until we moved to the US in 1995. It wasn't all that hard for me to start over with two small kids and my husband driving our only car, because we found a church immediately that did a fantastic job of supporting us in any way it could. What was difficult was the work we had to do on ourselves in the marriage in order to stay connected and open with each other. We both worked our way through the independent stage, but it took about fifteen years to get ourselves to the settled stage. Once that was over, we decided to take a risk and go after some of our many hopes and dreams. We were ready to invest all we had into them. And we did. *All we had.* We both failed and were let down in painful ways. We survived.

There's something about losing everything that brings great peace. It's as if once you lose everything you were afraid of losing, you realize that your fear was magnified way beyond what it's actually like to walk through it. God never left us, and time after time he came through for us through connections, gifts, and opportunities.

So many things can set everything into a tailspin—accidents, divorces, addictions, foreclosures, health issues, job losses. We stand with the greats. Job lost his wealth, his health, and children (Job). Joseph's brothers betrayed him, and he was thrown into a prison in Egypt for years (Genesis 37–50). Moses went from being an Egyptian ruler to being a shepherd for forty years (Exodus). The disciples gave up everything to follow Jesus and then he was murdered before their eyes (the Gospels). Yet their lives were not over. Their glory days had only just begun. *What if your glory days have only just begun?*

These days my husband and I float quite easily between the settled and legacy stages of life. We don't feel the urgency to do something spectacular with our lives because that's not all that important to us anymore. What's important is that we are faithful in being *us* every day—valuing each other, valuing and helping others, being kind, laughing, growing in character, developing our skills further, and being more and more in tune with God. Surprisingly, the more we chill out about how we look to the world, the more we seem to be able to invest in other people's lives. Life is good these days.

What may appear to be the wrong way by other people's standards may indeed be the perfectly inspired path by which you will arrive at clarity of mind and a more authentic expression of yourself."
~ Linda Cull, Where the Light Lives: A True Story about Death, Grief and Transformation

THINK IT THROUGH, FIGURE IT OUT

It often helps to have visuals so we can carry pictures in our minds of how our lives are, so below is a timeline of Cinderella's story, followed by an empty timeline for you to fill.

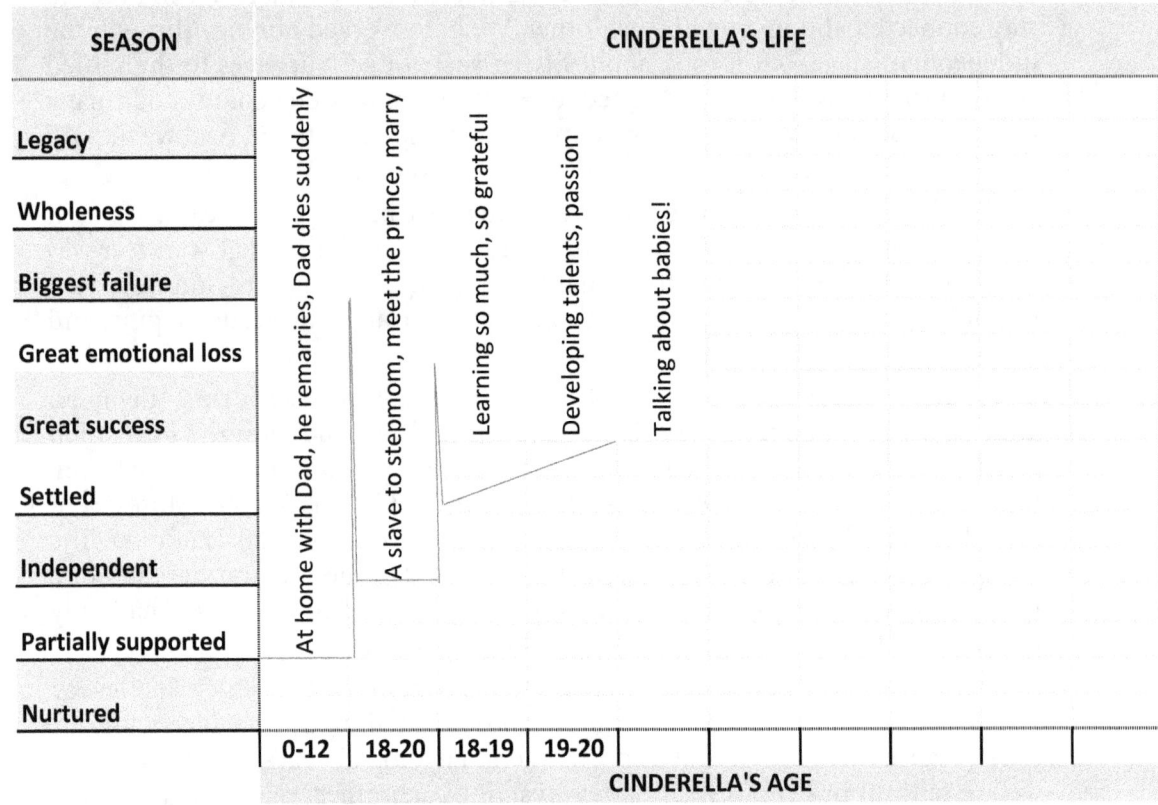

Cinderella's story would go something like this:

I never knew my mother, but my father made up for that with his unconditional love and encouragement every day. My safe, beautiful world changed drastically when he married a very broken woman who saw me as an enemy, and I almost wanted my life to end completely when he died suddenly when I was twelve. I was alone and abandoned, but I felt God everywhere, talking to me through nature and giving me hope to go on. I quickly learned how to follow my stepmother's rules and do things with excellence, and I felt that obeying her was the safest way to live.

I began to see what my life could be like outside the house through the books

I read in my dad's library. And when the news came that the prince was hosting a ball for everyone, I knew that for the first time ever, I was willing to take a risk and be there.

It was worth every minute of fear, and when my fairy godmother showed up to help, I saw I'd never been alone all those years after all—and never would be.

Now I'm a queen, I can see how all those years of slavery and obedience have served me well. I know how to lead well, how to expect excellence through encouragement, how to walk with confidence. I know I am here to serve a kingdom and be a role model for every young woman.

I'm even taking singing lessons and teaching the cooks how to experiment with unusual ingredients I bring back from our travels. It's so great to see their eyes light up with excitement over it.

I'm not afraid anymore. I have a voice now. I'm excited about the future and what my husband and I can do together to make this kingdom great again. I love this life.

MY LIFE STORY

SEASON	MY LIFE
Legacy	
Wholeness	
Biggest failure	
Great emotional loss	
Great success	
Settled	
Independent	
Partially supported	
Nurtured	

MY AGE

FINISH THESE SENTENCES

When I look back at my life journey so far, I think

When I look at my life so far through God's eyes, he sees

My favorite season in life was when

When I look for the gold I can take from my most difficult season, I can see

My relationship with others has changed over the years to become

My relationship with God has changed over the years to become

TRUTH

What is the truth about your life journey? Mull over the following Scriptures and write down anything God shows you through them.

> "Then all the congregation raised a loud cry, and the people wept that night. And all the people of Israel grumbled against Moses and Aaron. The whole congregation said to them, 'Would that we had died in the land of Egypt! Or would that we had died in this wilderness! Why is the Lord bringing us into this land, to fall by the sword? Our wives and our little ones will become a prey. Would it not be better for us to go back to Egypt?'" (Numbers 14:1–3)

> "Moses was 120 years old when he died. His eye was undimmed, and his vigor unabated." (Deuteronomy 34:7)

> "All these are the twelve tribes of Israel. This is what their father said to them as he blessed them, blessing each with the blessing suitable to him." (Genesis 49:28)

> "Paul thanked God and took courage. ... He [Paul] lived there two whole years at his own expense, and welcomed all who came to him." (Acts 28:15–16,30)

LISA'S JOURNEY (EARLY FIFTIES)

I sometimes joke that descriptive phrase in *The Poky Little Puppy* could sum up my life: roly-poly, pell-mell, tumble-bumble. From conception my story seemed random and bumpy—like a second-rate author on his third whiskey was making it up as he went along.

My mother immigrated to the US (Minnesota) from Germany, married a man of Greek descent, before she ran away with a singer on his way to Chicago—where she met another Greek (newly arrived) who booked singers for a nightclub, before she continued on with the original singer to CBS studios in L.A.—where I was born. It took a decade and a DNA test to figure out where I was conceived and by which singer or by which Greek.

On the surface, all of this sounds as if it's random, but it isn't.

I was six months old when my mother paid a stewardess to fly with me to Germany to live with my grandmother. Not random. My mother married when I was four, and her new husband, Richard, an abusive alcoholic, thought my grandmother should bring me back to the States. Richard didn't let my mother speak German with me. Not random. I lived with them until I was eight, when social workers placed me under the guardianship of a nearby Brazilian family of gifted artists.

Not random.

At eighteen, I joined the US Army requesting an assignment in Germany so I could see my grandmother again, who had not been told about all the years I was with guardians. At nineteen I became a serial dater until I met "Chuck"—a Christian who taught me what the characteristics of goodness looked like, sounded like, felt like. Not random. I applied and was accepted to the Defense Language Institute to relearn my first language—which wouldn't have happened if Richard had allowed me to speak German with my mother. Not random. I met and fell in love with Sam, a Korean linguist who was a good man, a fact I recognized because of "Chuck." Not random.

Upon graduating, I went to Germany for my assignment and to spend time with my family. Sam came to visit on his way to South Korea. Of all the times I could have gotten pregnant—that's when it happened. Sam's response: Hey! I'm going to be a father! I was glad he felt confident about parenthood, because I had no idea what I was going to do. We got married in Seoul but settled down in a village. Day after day, I watched Korean mothers and grandmothers caring—I mean *really* caring for their children. Besides teaching me about motherhood, I had the opportunity to be a bridge—helping to connect Korean and American wives on base. Not random.

Fast forward back to the States to rural Virginia. Various parts of who I was continued to collide. I found a group of Christian homeschooling mothers and accepted the call to homeschool. At about that time, I took some college writing courses and a class called "Building Bridges Not Walls." It had a profound impact. I became a liaison, connecting the Catholic homeschool group with the Protestant homeschool group. We came together for events, learning, prayer, and fellowship.

I began writing again.

Then my mother died.

It was the first time I remember being angry at God. I thought I'd have time with her after Richard died—he'd had two strokes and wasn't in great health. But Richard was deeply broken. A social worker said they could put him in a state-run home. I brought Richard home. Before he died, Richard asked me if I knew anything about my biological father. At that point, I didn't. He told me what he knew: Minnesota to Chicago to L.A. to the singers and the Greeks. That started me on the search that would end with the name Petropoulos and give me three brothers and a sister (among other family) in Chicago.

In the meantime, I'd put together a collection of short stories, *Her Safari*. The publisher asked me to make a promo-video for it and turn one of the short stories into a short film. Making the first short film added a dimension to my storytelling that had been waiting in the wings most of my life—the visual, artistic dimension. I wrote a full-length screenplay next. A cinematographer from L.A. was on the East Coast looking for a project. He picked mine. Two years later, *SPENT* had a one-week theatrical release in Hollywood—minutes from CBS studios where my mom was working when I was born.

I was thirty when I came to an initial understanding of who God is, which in turn led me to read the Bible. What struck me over and over and over was how God is a god of time and place. Even when events seem to be random, they aren't. It's no accident the Good Samaritan was on that road at that time.

The time in Germany with my grandmother gave me a foundation. The return to America served to expand my thoughts, my heart. My time with the family from South America and my time in Asia allowed me to walk in so many different shoes and see life from many different angles. It's allowed me to be a bridge in my daily life between various kinds of people and personalities. It's allowed me to be salt and light because I understand that life is hard—compassion was woven into me. But life is also beautiful, and I was equipped to share some of that beauty. My purpose in life isn't to write or to make movies—it's to connect with the people who cross my path and show them something of who God is.

When we meet, Jesus is there, and I will know without a doubt that our meeting isn't random, what we talk about isn't random, and what it leads to isn't random.

Because nothing about God, the Creator of life and moments, is random.

https://www.imdb.com/name/nm7039377

Notes

Notes

ACTION 11

"Have you been called to the ministry of Christian counseling?" This piece of junk mail rocked my world in 2003. Knowing I was disqualified to ever be in ministry, God began a healing process that has led to a Christian counseling ministry, touching lives and bringing healing to others through Jesus. I've been living my dream for fourteen years.
~ Al J.

Desperation made me take action. Loss of self. I needed to find myself again, tap into creative outlet that would reconnect me with the person I was before. A friend suggested I write a book, somewhat jokingly. It went from a thought to an urge, and so I sat down and wrote it. My book will be out in one month.
~ Negeen P.

When I was seventeen, my parents heard about my dreams. They meant well; don't get me wrong. They just, you know, didn't want me to be a starving artist. So they steered me in a different direction, which is how I wound up with a bachelor's in criminal justice and a career as a flight attendant. I suddenly realized that if I was still working a dissatisfying job when I was thirty, it would be my fault and no one else's. So I decided to spend every spare minute of my twenties making my dream a reality. Just because it takes years to make strides toward living the dream doesn't mean it's not worth the effort.
~ Rebecca T.

I have wanted to be a professional photographer for many years, and last year I gave permission to have some of my photographs published online. This year I have already spent a number of weekends improving my skill, and I plan to have many more publishable works by the end of the year.
~ Marc W.

I got ideas in my head of what my life was, and then the Lord said what I thought about my life, direction, and calling was different to what he saw. I had a decision to make about that.
~ Peggy R.

When people come to me for a coaching session, it's usually because they're stuck and want to move forward into better things. They know that complaining about their circumstances hasn't changed anything, and while some of them have incredibly hard circumstances that aren't going to change anytime soon, there's more to their lives than that one big thing people keep telling them they've been put on earth to do.

God would agree. We were not designed to be one-trick ponies. There isn't only one purpose to our being here. We're made up of so many great parts, and those parts flow through each year of our lives to be served up wherever they are needed with our unique flavors. Some people have spent decades developing their knowledge and experience, like Dave Ramsey, who has turned his experience in handling household finances into a teaching empire. Hundreds of thousands of people are debt free because of his willingness to invest in the best ways of bringing that to a large audience. Others are amazing at keeping their core and extended families connected, and they live for the days when all the generations are together. Others have a passion for community development and spend their days researching, learning, reading, and finding solutions for problems that affect everyday life.

Sadly, shame over what they're not doing cripples so many. The one area many people instantly express shame over is the area of personal health—physical and mental. I should eat healthier food. I should see a counselor. I should work out so much I have a six pack for the rest of my life. But shame is not good currency. You can't set it on the counter and get something great in exchange. Decision, however, is. Every choice is a step out of living the kind of life you don't want and into the kind you do. I think that part of what keeps people trapped in cycles of shame is that they've already tried to change and failed; and that failure was enough to prevent them from trying again.

Most of the great Bible characters we've grown up hearing about experienced great failure. Moses failed miserably. I don't think you can get much worse than murder. Gideon kept refusing to obey God because he was terrified he wasn't the guy God thought he was. Duh. Peter, after professing his undying love and then getting affronted at Jesus saying he'd deny him, failed spectacularly; and his promises came out of his lips so easily. But *they all got up and tried again, because even though they didn't believe in themselves, they knew God believed in them.* God knows what he's made. He knows what you're capable of. He knows that if you're open to hear him cheer you on, no matter how many times you fall, you can reach each goal and stay there.

Another thing that deters people from pushing on is the fear that they're not worth the work. Who am I that…? Don't question why God made you. Accept that he did and roll with it. Being the best *you* you can be starts with being whole in spirit, but what closely follows is being whole in soul and body as well. No matter what you're afraid of, no matter what lies you believe about yourself, no matter what you think your worth is, God is bigger. He is enough, He's holding out everything you need to be fully alive and fully you, and he doesn't expect it to happen overnight. Seriously, know that when you're living in the center of life and wholeness, you're in the center of everything you need to *be*.

The valley in Psalm 23 is only the valley of the *shadow* of death. All fear and lies are shadows of things that might happen but probably won't. You see huge shadows when you stand with your back to the sun, but if you face the sun and walk forward in light and truth, the shadows will remain at your back to eventually disappear. All the devil has to pull you away from living in light and truth, from living up to your full potential, is that fear and those lies. You can choose which way to face. We can't let our fear of the unknown supersede our faith. I've seen far too many people miss out on great opportunities because they're afraid of things like suffering physical pain, failing, or being rejected. It's true that some decisions taken in faith will end up making life much more difficult for a while, but either you trust God or you don't. He either has your heart or he doesn't. He'll either carry you through anything or he won't. If you're going to live life fully alive, you need to deal with this fear factor. You need to accept that bad things might happen, accept that God is always with you in every situation in life, and decide that's enough for your heart.

> *To be honest, being in control is a joke anyway. When was the last time God did something exactly the way you expected?*

God's main gift to us is not our personal happiness; it's that we get to be an integral part of the bigger plan—to give life and give it abundantly. That includes what we learn by pushing past our fears and tasting all life has to give. How do you eat an elephant? One bite at a time. It's the same with moving forward and climbing out of the slough you're in. Either way, it's time to move. You don't have to grow everything at once. It took Jesus three years to give his disciples some wisdom and understanding. It took Boaz years to find a good wife, and even then, God had to practically push her in his face to get him to notice her. Accomplish small things that move you further along the road toward realizing a fuller, more life-filled life. Just get on with it and forget about a timeline unless God's given you a specific one. God believes in you. I believe in you. Now get cracking!

PERSONAL ASSESSMENT

What I have below is my own version of a pie chart you have probably seen many times, because it's such a practical took in assessing where you're at in life vs. where you want to be. In each triangle or piece of the pie, score yourself—out of ten—how satisfied you are with that part of your life. Once you've got a score in each part, you'll see which areas of your life need some help and which you are doing quite well in.

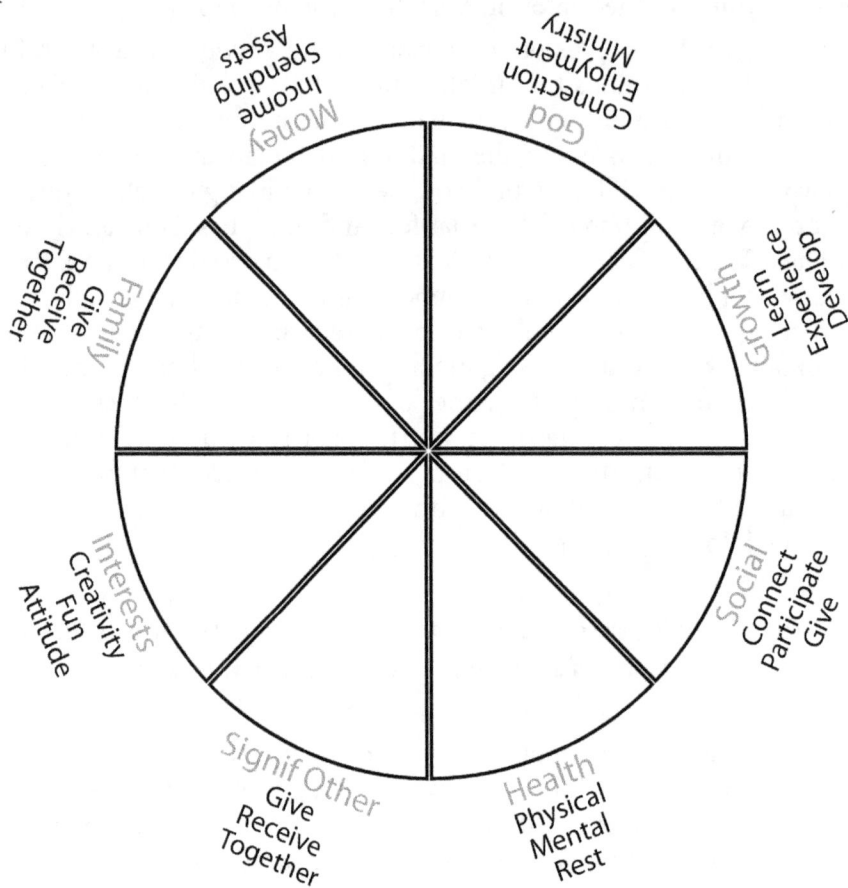

If you tie these numbers with your ideals vs. values form, you'll probably see some similarities in that the things you've given time to are in better shape than the ones you've said were important but ignored, for the most part. Even now, as you decide to start an action plan, you'll probably veer toward improving the areas you have a higher value for.

Below, write down your top three areas you'd like to work on, followed by what would look like wholeness to you. For example, if you'd like to improve your personal growth, then write Growth—I'd spend time learning about all the things I don't understand from factually based sources like books and speakers with experience and wisdom. I'd develop my speaking skills. I'd spend more time listening to people outside my social bubble.

1.

2.

3.

Now you have the big picture in place, it's time to narrow it down to the first step. This is where the perfectionists and overachievers jump with excitement, especially those in their more youthful years. They write something like: This week, I'm going to check out five books from the library on the color red and read them all by Sunday. It's not going to happen. The most important thing about your first steps is that they have to be achievable and factor in any emotional or scheduling weaknesses you may have. A more realistic step would be to check out one book and have the first chapter read by Sunday by reading one page a night after dinner. What will your first actionable step be for the area you're least happy with? Follow it with one doable step for the next two areas as well.

1.

2.

3.

Taking action like this will raise you out of the depths and put your mind back into regular life again. Once you accomplish those three first small steps, you make three more, until you're back up to a level you're fairly satisfied with. If it's growth, hopefully you're in tune enough with God to where you're not now acting like a know-it-all....

FINISH THESE SENTENCES

I want/don't want to move forward because

If I move forward, the outcome could be

The percentage in which I trust God to be with me and hold me as I move forward in things I'm afraid of is ___ %.

I think it will take me ___ years to _____ because

I would like to start taking action by

Jesus thinks my hopes and plans are

TRUTH

What is the truth about taking action? Mull over the following Scriptures and write down anything God shows you through them.

"Faith by itself, if it does not have works, is dead." (Philippians 1:6)

"The Lord said to Moses, 'Why do you cry to me? Tell the people of Israel to go forward.'" (Exodus 14:15)

"Fear not, for I am with you; be not dismayed, for I am your God; I will strengthen you, I will help you, I will uphold you with my righteous right hand." (Isaiah 41:10)

"And we desire each one of you to show the same earnestness to have the full assurance of hope until the end, so that you may not be sluggish, but imitators of those who through faith and patience inherit the promises." (Hebrews 6:11–12)

"Arise, for it is your task, and we are with you; be strong and do it." (Ezra 10:4)

DORIS'S JOURNEY (EARLY SEVENTIES)

I was the last of three children of two deaf parents. We were all seven years apart, so I played by myself a lot. I could make myself happy for hours on end with my imagination. I knew Christ as a child. I always knew he was with me and he was love. I'd always seen darkness and, occasionally, some angels. I always knew Jesus as the man in the long white clothes. Even the kids in Thailand will say, who's that man in the long dress, the long white dress? Why does that man have a dress on?

When I was three, we got hit by a train and my dad screamed. I'd never heard my dad speak, and that scared me more than getting hit by the train! We rolled over and over, down into the bayou. We had no seat belts back then. Then this skinny dude came up, picked me up—right out of the truck—and he didn't walk up the bank; he put me on the top of the bank. It was five hundred feet away, and then he worked for about five minutes. He picked up my daddy and put him on top of the bank, and then our truck blew up and burned to nothing. We couldn't find the guy anywhere.

I had a wonderful childhood. I was always loved, and my father and I had the best relationship. He always told me to never pay attention to people's words, because living them was what counted. My parents taught me that if you worked hard and didn't make people mad, you could get anywhere you wanted in life. The trick was to just be agreeable ... but inside me was a passion to make wrongs right. I tended to always push against the stream.

I never thought we were poor. I thought everyone ate popcorn on Friday nights, and we were like the local social services, before that was a thing. My grandfather and my dad would help deaf people and we always had food, thanks to the local farms, to give to people who had none.

My first job was when I was ten. I washed dishes or babysit for 15–26 cents an hour, and I saved enough to go to beauty college—$120 worth. I went when I was eleven, put my money down on the table, and said, "I want to do this." I was one of the youngest people to ever get her license at sixteen. I won hairstyling awards. After I got married, my mother-in-law forced me to let my husband get his degree first. I never got mine. I worked and I had a baby and then I had the second baby. And then I got called.

Jesus came into my room as I was getting ready to leave my husband. We were having marital problems. I had the kids' clothes packed. I had my own clothes packed. I had cleared all the money out of the bank accounts. I had his passport—he wasn't going anywhere. I was mad. He was drunk every night, going out dancing, coming home with lipstick on his collar, wasn't treating me nice. I'd had it. I thought *Buddy, I'm getting even*. I said, "God, I'm leaving you too. I'm giving you one last chance to prove to me that you're real." Jesus appeared in my room and talked to me from his eyes. He said, "Would you work with my people?" and I knew he meant deaf people. I thought *Oh, God, that's a lot of work. I don't want to do this.* He asked me again and I said yes, and then he poured what felt like honey on the top of my head. It went into my bones. I looked at my husband and I was immediately maddeningly in love with him again. I looked at Jesus and said, "This is the most unfair thing you have ever done to me! He has been a jerk! Do you do this to everybody you know?" I was totally in love with Jesus after that encounter, and my life did a one-eighty. The very next day practically all the deaf people in the county ran into me, saying I was the one they'd been looking for for two years because they knew I could sign and understand what they were saying. That's how I became an interpreter.

An angel came one day and took me to show me where the brothels were with the children. I went with him and saw the Thai people I loved going into the brothels to have sex with the kids. I was in shock. I couldn't believe it. The angel said, "Come on." I said, "Wait a minute. I can't go right now. I'm in shock." He looked at me like *You fool,* and the angel brought me back to my house and dropped me off at my door. Jesus was standing there and said, "You have not obeyed, and I cannot stop your consequences, but I will be with you through the consequences." It looked like I'd been bitten by a *paranak*—an eight-headed snake. Having shingles was the most painful experience of my life, and I was full of fear. I wrote down everything I was afraid of, and then God led me to the Bible verses that gave me the answers to my fears. I wrote out a prayer of surrendering to God and who he said I was, and whenever I read it, it would take the pain away.

My greatest success has been my surrender to Jesus Christ in Thailand and receiving his baptism of love in my twenties. It's a perpetual baptism in the love that I have for everyone. I am here to bring all the glory to God and to catch and release people into the power of God and the love of Jesus. I catch them and love them. I've been blunt all my life, but in Thailand I learned my identity. I needed to find out how God saw me. I knew he was the one I needed to agree with about who I was and now I haven't had a mask in years. I don't even need to impress the president these days.

I don't believe I'm ever my best self, and I don't think I ever will be. That can only happen when he's the greatest in me, but I get in the way. Every night Jesus comes to me. He manifests on my side of the bed, or an angel does, and there's so much light sometimes I have to cover my eyes. We talk about everything, and he tells me what he wants. I'm happy for my life to fulfill what he wants me to fulfill in a way that's pleasing to him. I'm doing my best as his beacon on a hill.

After I'm gone, I want people to be intimate with Jesus. If they're not, my life was a waste and all those words were in vain.

Notes

Notes

Legacy 12

My deep desire is that those who come after me wouldn't have to start over but can begin with a foundation of my thirty years of lessons, mistakes, and stories of breakthrough and see even more victories than I ever imagined!

~ Cindy J.

I want to leave a legacy of love and passion for service.

~ Sarah D.

I want to impart a sense of wonder and respect in children for the people who care for them, for God, and for the world we live in during the most formative years. I hope to give them the tools to get through life without causing themselves extra pain and misfortune, to be fascinated with learning, and to have an overwhelming desire to experience the rich tapestry of the human condition. And finally, I want to gift to them a set of skills: 1) respect for the elders that love and keep them safe, 2) a basic understanding of what the weather and nature offer and how to interact with them, and 3) how to work in the kitchen to create food for themselves and others.

~ Tracey L.

I want to have always encouraged those around me. I want to have listened more than I spoke, and I want to have made all the people in my life feel they were important and cherished.

~ Abigail P.

I want people to say they saw Jesus through me.

~ Belinda S.

I'm writing biblical teaching curriculum for adults. I ghostwrite it so only the Lord knows what my legacy is worth, and I trust him with it.

~ Birdie C.

I hope to create a legacy of disciplined work, independent thinking, and self-sacrifice.

~ Jamie F.

While the correct definition of the word "legacy" means an amount of money or property left to someone in a will, we've come to associate the word with more than just monetary value. I touched on the subject of legacy in the journey chapter, saying when you get to the place in life when you are focused on leaving a legacy:

YOU are your best self, completely comfortable in your own skin.

YOU don't need to impress anyone.

YOU'RE a light on a hill.

YOU serve others well with your lifetime of walking with God, knowledge, people skills, and experience.

YOU'RE happy to have lived a fulfilling life and are paving the way for others to live well.

I love the way Jacob did this—he called all the sons together, called out each one's unique design, and blessed them with more of that goodness. Well ... some he didn't say anything nice about. He mustn't have read *The Five Love Languages* or heard about love sandwiches. Maybe they just rattled his cage one too many times.

I'm middle-aged now, and over the years I've come to see what's really worth holding onto vs. what runs through my fingers and disappears, leaving no lasting value. I want to see people's lives become more whole because of mine. That's what fills me with joy and that assuredness of doing what I was born for. Will I win brownie points in heaven for accomplishing some of these dreams? Nope. God doesn't work on a point system. His chief focus is: Do we know God's love? Are we sharing God's love? His love is *it*.

Our lives can be constantly developing, flourishing, growing ever closer to being filled with the love and attitude of Jesus. Society would tell us that we'll never achieve that level of success, that no one will ever know our names. So what? *No one needs to know your name. But they do need to know your heart.* What they need to know is Jesus in you, and you can reflect him best when you are fully you, living life fully alive in him. Yes, a small percentage of your state or country might end up knowing your name because people talk. And if they love you because you fill a need in their lives for love, information, support, or joy, then you've served them well. You've done *you* well.

Many years ago we flew home to be with my dad who was dying from cancer. I was trying to think of what I could give him for his last Christmas. What do you give the man who has raised you and loved you unconditionally? What do you say when you know it will be the last time you get to talk with him? A God idea came to me—what if I let him know his personal legacy to me *before* he died?

What if I printed it out and framed it so he could read it whenever he wanted? As I wrote, it became clear to me that his legacy was himself. A piece of him had lodged itself in me, and I carry his story forward. His way of being, how he served with his dreams and passion and gifts and skill set, his ongoing decisions to move forward no matter how bad things got, and his love for us all—all six children and my mother—made us more complete.

This is what our legacies will be too. Pieces of us have been and will be lodged in hearts as deposits of heaven, gifts that can be paid forward. I can already hear the voices in your head laughing. Gift from heaven? Yes, you are a gift to this world. Sure, there are probably some parts of you you'd rather not see sticking around, but that's the beauty of death: we're all instant saints when they get up to talk about us at the funeral.

Jesus knew what his legacy would be, to include perfect peace, fullness, wholeness, oneness, and unconditional love. "Peace I leave with you; my peace I give to you. Not as the world gives do I give to you" (John 14:27). "Now they know that everything that you have given me is from you" (John 17:7). "For their sake I consecrate myself, that they also may be sanctified in truth" (v.19). "The glory that you have given me I have given to them, that they may be one even as we are one, I in them and you in me, that they may become perfectly one, so that the world may know that you sent me and loved them even as you loved me" (v. 22–23). The incredible thing about his legacy is that we don't just get pieces of Jesus; *we get all of him.*

Jesus was the true model of what an excellent legacy looks like. He was his best self, completely comfortable in his own skin; didn't need to impress anyone; was a light on a hill; served others well with his lifetime of walking with God, knowledge, people skills, and experience; was delighted to have lived a fulfilling life; and was paving the way for others to live well. His life showed us all what's possible when we're one with God. His death made that possible.

I asked God once about the verse about building up treasures in heaven. It seemed a bit weird to think that I'd earn jewels along the journey and get to open the treasure chest once I got my special room. He said that every time I helped someone feel loved, supported, or encouraged, I was building up his treasures—*his people.*

THIS is what God considers valuable. This is what we are here for. How we serve up us + God will be our legacies.

ARE you ready?

PULLING IT ALL TOGETHER

Your body, soul, and spirit are happily coming back to life. You don't feel like a useless failure anymore because look—you read a chapter, you were nice to your partner five days in a row, and you finally called your mother. You're present, you're getting stuff done, and you're living life on purpose; and once you figure out the whole package of *you* God had in mind, you can live life *in* your purpose too by simply *being* in him.

It's time to pull everything you've done in this book together. I love this part. It's where God gets to pull the thread of all his sewing to create our pleats and ruffles.

MY DESIGN:

What do I think God's blueprint was for me?

MY MIRROR:

What does God see when he looks at me vs. what I see in the mirror?

MY PERSONALITY:

My DISC profile says I am

My Type in Mind profile says I am

God gave me this personality on purpose because/so

GIFTS AND TALENTS:
God made my top natural gifts and talents

KNOWLEDGE AND EXPERIENCE:
The knowledge and experience God has helped me gain lie mostly in

SPIRITUAL GIFTS:
The top spiritual gifts God has given me are

VALUES:
My top values are

PASSION:
God has made me most passionate about

My niche sentence about myself is (p.100): I accomplish

FEAR:

My biggest fears about fulfilling my life purpose are:

God says

LIFE JOURNEY:

When I look back at my life journey with God in relation to living out my purpose, I see

LEGACY

DREAMS:

I dream of

ACTION:

God wants me to

FINISH THESE SENTENCES

The greatest parts of my relationship with God that I would most like people to carry forward are

The character qualities God has grown in me throughout my life journey that I would most like people to carry forward are

If I believe God and see myself as a valuable part of other people's lives every day, here's what I'm going to do differently:

My first small step into doing that will be

Jesus says my legacy will be

TRUTH

What is the truth about your legacy? Mull over the following Scriptures and write down anything God shows you through them.

"But lay up for yourselves treasures in heaven, where neither moth nor rust destroys and where thieves do not break in and steal. For where your treasure is, there your heart will be also." (Matthew 6:20–21)

"And now there remain: faith [abiding trust in God and His promises], hope [confident expectation of eternal salvation], love [unselfish love for others growing out of God's love for me], these three [the choicest graces]; but the greatest of these is love." (1 Corinthians 13:13 AMP)

"'Which commandment is the most important of all?' Jesus answered, 'The most important is, "Hear, O Israel: The Lord our God, the Lord is one. And you shall love the Lord your God with all your heart and with all your soul and with all your mind and with all your strength." The second is this: "You shall love your neighbor as yourself." There is no other commandment greater than these.'" (Mark 12:28–33)

"His gifts to the church were varied ... [and He did this] to fully equip and perfect the saints ... to build up the body of Christ [the church]; until we all reach oneness in the faith ... [manifesting His spiritual completeness and exercising our spiritual gifts in unity]." (Ephesians 4:11–13 AMP)

Odyssey is the perfect word for life, because our lives are long, often wandering trips marked by self-discovery and many changes of circumstances. An odyssey is also a quest, though, and we search incessantly for that missing, key part of our lives—something great and dramatic we could do if we just knew what it was. That thing, that life purpose, would define us and help us leave the world knowing we had done our "thing." But you're already defined as *you*. When you're one with God, you don't need to do anything else to be complete. You have the peace the world cannot give, a "being in Christ" peace rather than a "doing everything right" peace. You'll succeed and fail, you'll gain and lose, you'll rejoice and weep, and you'll get to be fully you *in him* in every one of those moments.

Do you well *in him*.

That's enough. That's the challenge. That's your purpose.

A DECLARATION (BASED ON EPHESIANS 4)

Declare out loud:

Thanks to the freely given power of Christ, I can walk in a manner worthy of the calling to which I have been called, with all humility and gentleness, with patience, bearing with others in love, eager to maintain the unity of the Spirit in the bond of peace.

Grace was given to me according to the measure of Christ's gift.

Jesus has designed us all and given us all gifts to build each other up until we all attain to the unity of the faith and of the knowledge of the Son of God, to mature manhood/womanhood, to the measure of the stature of the fullness of Christ.

I can grow up in every way into him who is the head, into Christ, from whom the whole body, joined and held together by every joint with which it is equipped, when each part is working properly, makes the body grow so that it builds itself up in love and encourages everyone to come into a heart-to-heart relationship with the Father.

Your life purpose is to be fully alive and whole in God, fully you, immersed in his love. The more you live in him and from him, the more faith, hope, and love will pour from you. You are a true demonstration of what's possible when our hearts and minds are one with God's.

Notes

NOTES

ABOUT THE AUTHOR

Sally Hanan is an Irish import to the US. She made the eight-hour crossing back in the '90s with a husband and two young children in tow. Since then she has managed to mold her above-average kids (who are obviously absolute geniuses and extremely good-looking) into becoming acceptable adults, develop a powerful addiction to Facebook, and acquire more stuff than she knows what to do with.

On a more professional note, Sally has been counseling people for more than twenty-two years and is a certified life coach and a former facilitator at the Texas School of Supernatural Ministry. She also runs a writing and editing business on the side, because she gets bored easily and she loves fixing words as well as people.

Other Books by Sally

Fix Yourself is a workbook designed to help heal your heart and mind in God's presence so that you can move into emotional and spiritual wholeness. Each exercise encourages you to reflect on God's truth and then apply it. The truth is that there is nothing wrong with your original design, and in Jesus you will find everything you need to be restored to your unique and magnificent self. This book will help take you there, or at least help begin the journey. Because this is in workbook form, it can be adapted for use in small groups, with a mentor, or in workshops.

I really like this and will use it with my pastoral and inner healing teams. This is an amazing workbook that will be great for groups, individuals, and married people; with prayers, reflections, and work assignments that chart out inner change and help you to see God in the light of his love for you.
~ Shawn Bolz, Senior Pastor of Expression58
Author of *Translating God* and *God Secrets*

Empower Yourself in the Holy Spirit is a practical, step-by-step guide for living from heaven to earth. It equips believers to live plugged into the Holy Spirit. God wants us to know him, and we can be the conduit of his love, supercharged with all God's tools for purposeful living.

Learn how to activate and use the gifts through: Relationship—hear God's voice quickly and clearly through the world around you. Revelation—understand the messages God sends through visions, dreams, and prophetic words, and share his words in a healthy, uplifting way. Revolution—be a powerhouse of Holy Spirit gifts by giving love away through the arts, physical healing, and intercession. Reality - get comfortable sharing the gifts of the Holy Spirit with everyone in your everyday life. Flowing in the gifts of the Holy Spirit isn't just a nice idea or a thing you keep to yourself; it's a powerful way to share God's love with all of mankind.

A blind girl has a gift; a father's heart breaks; a young boy in Africa might die; the step-children want her dead husband's money … read these short snippets of fiction and be prepared to gasp, giggle, and groan. Sally Hanan's insight into the human heart brings a depth of richness to her stories, many of them written in a poetic style of prose that flows and gurgles like a country creek.

Her poignant crystal clarity of truth and honest point of view of meaning and simplicity gathers together in the smallest set of words for each short story .... These stories reminded me of just one word–HAIKU ....
~ Pierre Dominique Roustan,
author of *The Cain Letters*

Pastor Mike Schaefer is close to death from the life-threatening injuries of a skiing accident. His close, extended, and church families are determined to see him through. Joining forces to call on heaven and assail hell, they agree with one voice that he will not die but live to declare the works of the Lord. Read this emotional yet triumphant story of the faith of many and the day-to-day miracles of the God they serve.

I couldn't put it down! A great read.
~ Sandy Sheer, Co-pastor, Tulsa Church, Oklahoma

God's faithfulness to his Word and the power in it resounds throughout this book—one that is a true inspiration to us all.
~ Cindy Mansfield, Station Manager KNAT-TV/ SW Regional Manager, Trinity Broadcasting Network

www.ingramcontent.com/pod-product-compliance
Lightning Source LLC
Chambersburg PA
CBHW060459010526
44118CB00018B/2471